The Language of
Twentieth Century Music

The Language of
TWENTIETH CENTURY MUSIC

A Dictionary of Terms

By ROBERT FINK and ROBERT RICCI

Schirmer Books
A DIVISION OF MACMILLAN PUBLISHING CO., INC.
NEW YORK

Collier Macmillan Publishers
LONDON

Macmillan Publishing Co., Inc.
866 Third Avenue, New York, N.Y. 10022
Collier-Macmillan Canada Ltd.

First printing 1975

Printed in the United States of America

Library of Congress Cataloging in Publication Data

Fink, Robert. The language of twentieth century music.

Bibliography: p. 1. Music — Dictionaries. 2. Music — History and criticism — 20th century. I. Ricci, Robert, joint author. II. Title.

ML100.F55   780'.904   74-13308

ISBN 0-02-870600-5

Preface

This volume is intended for use by music students, music teachers on all levels, performers, writers on contemporary music, disc jockeys faced with deciphering arcane notes on record jackets, and perhaps a few curious souls who just like the music(s) of our time. It is evident from even a cursory survey that the basic terminology of twentieth century music has been grossly slighted in standard reference works. Most of the important terms in such areas as chance, electronic, and serial music and multimedia art can only be found in specialized books and periodicals, and the fields of jazz and rock are always separated from so-called serious music. As this volume comes to print there is an unprecedented interest in all of the kinds of music in our society. Hence, a comprehensive lexicon of twentieth century music seems both necessary and long overdue.

It is the purpose of this book to present the basic terminologies of chance music, computer music, electronic music, film music, jazz, musique concrète, multimedia, rock, twelve-tone music and other more traditional styles of composition (for a complete listing of musical styles included, see the appendix), as well as to mention a number of instruments and performance practices that have developed as composers have searched for new means of expression. Also, new tools for musical analysis have been included along with many of the important movements in contemporary plastic and graphic arts which employ techniques and aesthetic points of view similar to those found in twentieth century music.

Many difficult decisions had to be made concerning the inclusion and exclusion of terms. Voltage, envelope, and magnetic tape, for example, may on the surface seem out of place in a musical lexicon but are essential to the understanding of electronic music and hence were included along with a number of other technical terms from the field of electronics. Most of the terminology of traditional tonality was excluded. However, some familiar words such as transposition,

retrograde, and athematicism were included and given a new interpretation in the context of twentieth century musical practice. In
general, the criteria applied in the selection of terms were: 1. preva-
lence in the literature of and about music, and 2. usefulness in understanding some aspect of music. Undoubtedly there will be disagree-
ment as to the scope and focus of this book, but hopefully, as the first
volume of its kind, it will prove to be a valuable addition to musical
scholarship.

Our thanks go to many persons who offered encouragement for this
project and who read passages and offered constructive criticism. We
would like to mention Mr. William Allgood, Mrs. Janet Bogart, Dr.
Robert Holmes, and Dr. David Sheldon.

Kalamazoo, Michigan   ROBERT FINK and ROBERT RICCI

A Note on Cross References

An asterisk (*) indicates a cross-referenced term. If the term consists of more than one word, the asterisk follows the first word (e.g.,
analog* to digital computer or infra-diatonic* scale). A term is cross-
referenced only on its first appearance in an entry. The appendix lists
terms according to category and is intended to serve as an additional
form of cross-reference.

Contents

THE LANGUAGE

OF

TWENTIETH CENTURY MUSIC

A

A: Abbreviation for aggregate*.

absolute music: Music of a non-programmatic nature, lacking links to specific emotions, events, or characters.

abstract art: See abstract* expressionism, non-objective* art, cubism*, expressionism*, and action* painting.

abstract expressionism: A post-World War II art movement that has its roots in surrealism* and expressionism*. In painting, bright colors, large canvases, and bold strokes (usually having no reference to objective reality) are commonly found, along with an aesthetic very much concerned with the act of painting as well as with the finished product. Abstract expressionists often use unusual methods and tools to achieve their purpose. Notable painters connected with this movement are Mark Rothko, William Baziotes, Theodore Stamoz, and Richard Diebenkorn. See action* painting and non-objective* art.

acid rock: See psychedelic* rock.

acoustical guitar: Any non-electric guitar with a resonating sound box that uses either nylon or steel strings. Sometimes the acoustical guitar is called a Spanish or classical guitar.

action notation: A system of notation that indicates to the performer a course of action to pursue without actually indicating the specific result in sound. Noise events are handily dealt with using this notation, for example. The term was coined by Erhard Karkoschka in his book *Notation in New Music* (1966).

action painting: A movement that grew out of the abstract expressionist school of art in the decade from 1950-1960. Action painting stressed direct execution through movement and gesture. The paintings of Franz Kline, with bold sweeps of solid color masses jutting across the canvas, are exemplary of the spirit of action painting. The works of action painters are often huge (Kline's *Siegfried* is over eight feet high). Another outstanding action painter, Jackson Pollock, utilized the dripping, smearing, and splattering of paint instead of employing a more traditional application by brush or palette knife. Other notable action painters include Willem de Kooning and Robert Rauschenberg. Manifestations of this art movement in music are found in works of an essentially aleatoric* nature, having sporadic rhythms and melodic lines which create a collage* of sounds.

1

Composer John Cage was influenced by action painting, particularly through his friendship with Robert Rauschenberg.

adapted viola: An invention by composer Harry Partch which adds an extended fingerboard to a viola, creating thirty-seven stops to the octave. The string length is twenty inches from the bridge to the nut and the instrument is tuned in perfect fifths (G-D-A-E), an octave below the violin.

added-note chord: A tertian* harmony with one or more notes added to the basic structure. The D♮ on the third beat of the following example is an added note. The example is from *Piano Variations* (1930) by Aaron Copland.

added sixth: The interval of a major or minor sixth added above the root of a major or minor triad. In the following example the A is an added sixth:

added value: Composer Oliver Messiaen's term for the prolongation of a given rhythmic value by the addition of a dot. Any rhythm may be transformed in terms of its metric balance by the addition of a small value. The added value can be of any type, such as a note, a rest, or a dot that is added to another value. Of great importance to Messiaen is the fact that the addition of these elements completely changes the basic rhythmic feeling of the simpler pattern. The added value also

has the effect of transforming a given pattern into smaller note value units.

addition chord: A chord in which the frequency* of each note is the sum of the frequencies of the two notes immediately below. In equal temperament this relationship can only be approximated. Chords with more than five pitches are not possible, but given the limitless frequencies of electronic* music, additional chords of many different pitches can be constructed. The following example illustrates a five-pitch addition chord.

additive meter: A concept of meter in which the large metric unit is constructed by adding together various groupings of smaller rhythmic/metric units.

§ Could be designed as : ♪♪♪ ♪♪ ♪♪♪ (3 + 2 + 3); ♪♪♪ ♪♪♪ ♪♪ (3 + 3 + 2); or ♪♪ ♪♪♪ ♪♪♪ (2 + 3 + 3) instead of the more typical arrangement of ♪♪♪♪ ♪♪♪♪

adjacency: Refers to pitches that lie near one another. Often a structural significance is intended or implied.

aetherophone: See etherophone*.

aggregate: 1. General: any vertical combination of pitches (chord). 2. Set* theory: composer and theorist Milton Babbitt uses the term to identify vertical associations of hexachords* (or smaller segments) of combinatorial* sets. For example, the pitches of a hexachord of one set-form* will create a twelve-pitch aggregate with the pitches of a hexachord of a different set-form as long as there is no duplication of pitches between hexachords. See combinatoriality*. The following example, from Babbitt's *Three Compositions for Piano* (1947), illustrates **a**

twelve-pitch aggregate derived from the second hexachord of the given set-form.

ALEA: A specialized computer* program* devised by G. M. Koenig of the University of Bonn which functions as a subroutine* for generating a series of random numbers to be used in compositional processes.

aleaphone: An instrument made of inclined brass strips in a box. Metal balls are randomly dropped on the strips to produce sounds and roll off when a pedal levels the strips.

aleatoric: Adjective form of aleatory*.

aleatoric modulation: The random varying of a signal* by a narrow band of filtered white* noise. See filter*.

aleatory: This term pertains to the use of compositional processes and performance decisions that involve chance or randomness. Two examples are *Music of Changes* (1952) by John Cage, which was composed using chance* operations derived from the *I Ching*, and *Intersection 3* (1953) by Morton Feldman which introduces the element of randomness into the performance itself by leaving decisions concerning specific pitches, durations, and dynamic levels up to the performer. See chance* music.

Algerian scale: An eleven-note scale, containing two augmented seconds, that was used by Jacques Ibert in *Escales* (1924).

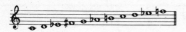

ALGOL: A programming* language that has been adopted widely as a common international language for the precise presentation of numeric procedures to a computer*. Many specialized computer programs in music rely on the ALGOL format to express information.

algorithm: A term from mathematics used to denote any special process or method used to solve a particular problem. In music involving mathematical processes of a high order the term applies when any special species of notation or calculation is developed toward a particular musical realization in sound. Mathematicians use the term to denote any method of computation, particularly one consisting of a small number of steps to be taken in a preassigned order moving toward the solution of a specific type of problem. The best-known example of an algorithm is Euclid's algorithm used to find the highest common factor of two given numbers. Algorithms play an important role in computing machines and hence computer* music.

all-combinatorial set: A twelve-tone* row constructed in such a way that the first six notes (hexachord*) of all of its transformations* at one or more levels of transposition* do not duplicate any of the first six notes of the original row. See combinatoriality*, semi-combinatorial* set. The row from Milton Babbitt's *Three Compositions for Piano* (1947) indicated below is combinatorial with the following set-forms*:

1. retrograde*; 2. prime* and retrograde transposed up an augmented fourth; 3. inversion* and retrograde-inversion* transposed up a minor second; 4. inversion and retrograde-inversion transposed up a perfect fifth.

all-interval series: See all-interval* set.

all-interval set: A specially constructed twelve-tone* row that contains all of the eleven possible basic intervallic relationships with no repetition. The following all-interval set is from *Canto Sospeso* (1956) by Luigi Nono.

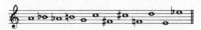

alphameric: See alphanumeric* notation.

alphanumeric notation: The use of a combination of letters and numbers to represent musical notation in a computer* program*.

altered chord: A tertian* harmony containing one or more notes which are chromatically foreign to the key or tonality.

AM: Abbreviation for amplitude* modulation.

ambience: Surrounding or environmental conditions such as the amount of natural light or sound present in a given situation. See ambient* noise.

ambient noise: The surrounding, environmental sounds present in any location or situation. Ambient noise is usually considered undesirable in tape* recording processes but may be desirable in the performance of certain avant-garde works.

ambit: The compass, range, or limits of some **parameter*** of music.

ambitus: See ambit*.

American Music Center: The American Music Center was founded in 1940 for the purpose of fostering and encouraging the composition of contemporary music by promoting its production, publication, distribution, and performance. The Center maintains a library with a collection of over 9,000 scores submitted by its member composers. These scores along with tape recordings are made available to conductors, performers, and scholars without charge. Other activities of the Center include the dissemination of biographical material, articles, and festival and competition information; and the listing of first performances, new recordings, and new publications in its newsletter *Music Today*.

American Society of Composers, Authors and Publishers: This organization was founded in 1914 by Victor Herbert, Raymond Hubbell, George Maxwell, and Nathan Burke in order to protect composers and their works from unfair exploitation. Copyright laws had been passed in 1897 whereby composers could collect damages for violation of copyright, but it was not until c. 1920 that ASCAP was a strong force in protecting its members.

American Society of University Composers: A professional organization of composers in American universities which held its first Annual National Conference in 1966. The Society was established to enable university composers to deal collectively with common problems and to foster awareness of contemporary musical thought and activity on campuses across the nation.

ametrical rhythm: Music utilizing free, non-metrically oriented patterns.

amplifier: An electronic device that changes the intensity or amplitude* of a signal*.

amplitude: 1. The compass of the complete vibratory cycle of a sound wave from mean position to maximum. 2. The loudness, intensity, or volume of a sound.

amplitude modulation: 1. General: the recurring boost and cut of the amplitude* of a sound wave. 2. Radio frequency*: varying the amplitude or intensity of a carrier wave in order to transmit a signal*. 3. Audio* frequency: varying the sound intensity or pressure level (loudness variation).

analog computer: An automatic electronic calculating machine that solves problems and processes data by using physical analogs such as shaft rotations or voltage* currents* to represent numerical variables. Results are conveyed as a graphic display such as an oscilloscope* pattern or as an electronic signal*.

analog signal: A signal* consisting of varying voltage*.

analog tape: Tape used to store information conveyed in a continuous flow of magnetic impulses. See magnetic* tape.

analog to digital conversion: The changing of analog* signals (data in varying voltage* form) to digital* signals (data in numerical or symbolic form) within a computer* network.

analysis-synthesis: Computer* analysis of the innate characteristics of a musical work followed by a compositional process that derives information from the analytic study. Lejaren Hiller's *Illiac Suite for String Quartet* (1957) is an example of a work formed through this process.

anechoic chamber: A room designed to eliminate all possible sound reverberation*.

anhemitonic music: 1. Music based on a scale of whole steps. 2. A scale or a set* that lacks semitones.

antimusic: The expression of ideas which negates the traditional concept of music. Works of antimusic may have no reference to sound in their scores, be impossible to perform, or break down the relationship between composer, performer, and audience. Two examples of antimusic are John Cage's *4'33"* (1952) which is a composition for silent piano and La Monte Young's *Composition 1960 #7* which consists of only two notes to be sustained for as long as possible. See dada*.

antirealistic art: Art movements in the twentieth century such as expressionism*, surrealism*, and other forms of abstractionism that have as their objective the negation of reality. See abstract* art and abstract* expressionism.

aperiodic vibrations: Irregularly occurring vibrations that do not conform to the natural harmonic* series.

arch form: A musical structure found frequently in the works of Béla Bartók which is characterized by themes or larger sections that reoccur in reverse order (e.g., ABCBA or ABCDCBA). Many times the apex of the arch (C or D) is devoted to the development of the materials of the other sections. Bartók's *Third* (1927), *Fourth* (1928), *Fifth* (1934) and *Sixth* (1939) *String Quartets* all include instances of arch form.

architectonic levels: The structural plateaus in a work upon which the form relies, creating unity, balance, and an interrelated quality among the smaller musical details. See Schenkerian* analysis, foreground*, middleground*, and background*.

ARP synthesizer: An electronic* music synthesizer* manufactured by the ARP instrument division of Tonus, Inc., in which modules* are interconnected primarily by sliding switches rather than by patch° chords. Sound production and modification instruments in this synthesizer are primarily activated by voltages° generated by a keyboard° controller, and a sequential° controller.

arrangement: A particular adaptation of a popular or standard° tune for a specific ensemble or performer. Hence a tune such as *Misty* (1954) by Erroll Garner could be conceived in an up-tempo jazz setting or as a slow ballad with full and lush instrumentation, depending upon the inclination of the musicians or the dictates of the performance setting.

array: An arrangement of a numerical series representing musical elements into a desired order or a geometric pattern such as a matrix°. In the following example of an array from *Structure Ia* (1952) by Pierre Boulez, the first horizontal line of numbers indicates the original form of the twelve-tone° row (See pitch° number). The second line represents a transposition° of the row beginning on the second note of the original. The third line represents a transposition of the row beginning on the third note and so forth. Diagonal lines drawn through the array were used to arrive at precise dynamic levels and modes of attack.

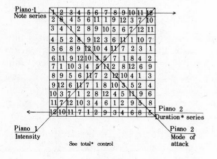

art deco: An American architectural movement of the late twenties and early thirties. Art deco had its roots in art nouveau°, cubism°, and American Indian art. As a style, art deco stressed symmetry and the straight line as opposed to curved and asymmetrical features. Perhaps the best example of art deco in this country is the Union Terminal (railroad station) in Cincinnati, Ohio. This structure covering an area of 287 acres features a half-dome 106 feet high. Two prominent artists, Winold Reiss and Pierre Bourdelle, decorated the terminal with mosaics, carved panels, and oil canvases glorifying labor and industry. In addition, Bourdelle decorated many areas with paintings and carvings heralding the beauty and exoticism of nature. The terminal was completed in 1933 and never realized the use for which it had been intended due to the gradual demise of railroads in the United States.

art nouveau: A late 19th and early 20th century form of artistic expression that was characterized by serpentlike curved lines derived from flowers and other elements of nature. Examples of this style are the ink drawings by Aubrey Beardsley found in Oscar Wilde's *Salome*.

ASCAP: Abbreviation for American° Society of Composers, Authors and Publishers.

athematicism: The absence of discernible themes in music, particularly the more familiar type of long-line theme found in music of the 18th and 19th centuries.

atonal: Adjective form of atonality°.

atonalism: The use of the concept of atonality° in composing music.

atonality: The absence of an evident tonal center (or centers) achieved through the avoidance of cadential patterns, tertian° chordal structures, and melodic sequences as found in tonal music. The term was first applied pejoratively by those opposed to compositions lacking any kind of key or tonal focus. Composer Arnold Schoenberg preferred the term pantonality* meaning a merging of tonalities. He pointed out that the term atonal was a misnomer because a literal translation would read "without tones".

atonical: Adjective form of atonicality*.

atonicality: An extension of tonality in which key centers are present, but no central "home key" is evident.

attack: See rise* time.

attack generator: See envelope* generator.

attack transients: See transient* overtones.

attenuation: The process of reducing the amplitude* (loudness) of a signal*.

attenuator: An electronic control that reduces the amplitude* of a signal*.

audio: A term that pertains to sound frequencies* within the range of human hearing and the electronic equipment involved in their transmission. Audio is a Latin word which can be translated as "I hear".

audio frequency spectrum shifter: An electronic device used to change all frequencies* up or down with the harmonics* remaining in the same relationship. The effect is a new pitch level with the same overtone* content as the original.

audio spectrum: The range of frequencies* discernible by the human ear.

audulator: An electronic device used to regulate the duration and frequency* with which a recorded sound is heard.

Augenmusik: German for eye* music.

augmentation: A compositional technique in which the duration values of a group of notes are increased by the same proportion. This is accomplished by adding to the value of each note in a group an equivalent amount such as twice the value, one-half the value, etc.

Ausfaltung: The unfolding of specific intervallic structures in Schenkerian* analysis. This process of horizontalism* is crucial to the organic development in a given work. See Urlinie*.

Auskomponierung: German for compositional* unfolding.

automatism: A process in musical composition consisting of the mechanical working-out of predetermined conditions in a work in which a number of parameters* are serialized*.

autonomous music: A term coined by Iannis Xenakis to denote a kind of internal conflict that exists in a given work between the printed form of the score and its actual sonic realization by the conductor and performers.

auto-polyphony: The creation of a polyphonic texture through the process of subjecting one melodic line to various methods of tape* manipulation.

auxiliary degree: Theorist Joseph Yasser's term for notes of a scale such as E and B in his infra-diatonic* scale that have a different role than that of the other notes; the auxiliary degrees being used for melodic embellishment in the form of nonharmonic or neighboring tones. In a diatonic scale the auxiliary degrees would be the five notes not used intrinsically as members of the scale, and in Yasser's supra-diatonic* scale the auxiliary degrees would roughly correspond to the notes of the regular diatonic scale.

avant-garde: Any art work or style which at a given point in time is considered to be experimental and/or advanced in technique.

axis relations: A term from the Schillinger* system used to denote the relationship between two or more strata, parts, or levels of a composition. For example, in a polyphonic work one would speak of the axis relationship between the independent melodic lines.

axis tone: A term used by theorist and composer George Perle to designate the specific note in a simultaneity* that carries the middle order* number of the twelve-tone* row.

B

background: The ultimate skeletal framework upon which the rest of a musical structure relies. See Schenkerian* analysis, foreground*, middleground*, and architectonic* levels.

bamboo marimba: A percussion instrument invented by composer Harry Partch in 1955 which is six feet broad at the base, four feet wide at the top, four feet tall, and has sixty-four bamboo keys. The instrument is played with felted sticks or small mallets and produces a dry, percussive sound in a range that extends from B♭ below middle C to F².

band: See frequency* band.

band-elimination filter: A filter* which severely attenuates* a specific band* of frequencies* while allowing other frequencies to pass through unaffected.

band-pass filter: A filter* which admits only a narrow band* of frequencies*. All frequencies above or below this band are attenuated* severely.

band-reject filter: See band-elimination* filter.

band-stop filter: See band-elimination* filter.

bandwidth: The specific frequency* range necessary for transmitting a given amount of information. See frequency* band.

bar breakdown: Information concerning a motion picture that is written on manuscript paper along with a graphic indication of a click* track. Bar breakdowns are used by film composers to plan the synchronization of music and film action. See film* music.

barrelhouse: A highly syncopated jazz* piano style common to saloons and gin mills in New Orleans around 1910. Barrelhouse is noted for its rough, vigorous, and unpolished flavor. See honky-tonk*.

BASIC: An acronym for Beginner's All-purpose Symbolic Instruction Code, which is a time-sharing* computer* programming* language for use with teletype terminals*. Many specialized computer programs in music use BASIC as a point of departure.

basic cell: A short, intervallically constant motive that can occur vertically or horizontally and can be varied through inversion*, retrograde*, retrograde-inversion*, and transposition*. A basic cell is used as a point of departure for larger set* relationships.

Bassbrechung: See Grundbrechung*.

bass guitar: A four-string guitar that reproduces the bottom four strings (E, A, G, and D) of the electric* guitar an octave lower.

bass marimba: An instrument built by composer Harry Partch in 1950 with a range from low cello C to B♭ below middle C. Its resonators are organ pipes fitted with tuning plungers, and the keys are made from Sitka spruce mounted on foam rubber. The instrument is played with a variety of mallets, bare hands, or wire cream whippers.

bebop: See bop*.

Bell Laboratories: Experimental laboratories owned jointly by the American Telephone and Telegraph Company and Western Electric where early research was done in tape* recording and computer* sound-generation.

bend: A slow, downward slur applied to a tone in jazz.

bichord: A vertical* sonority consisting of two simultaneous identifiable chord structures (e.g., triads or seventh chords). See polychord*. The following example indicates a bichord formed from an F major triad and a B major triad:

bi-chromatic: Music based on the use of quarter* tones as opposed to half and whole steps.

big band: A jazz* ensemble consisting of twelve to thirty players made up of brasses (typically trumpets, trombones, and flugelhorns), reeds (saxophones and clarinets), and rhythm instruments (drums, string bass, guitar, piano, and vibraphone). See neophonic* orchestra, swing*.

bimeter: The simultaneous use of two different meters. The following example from the third movement of *Kammermusik Nr. 2* (1925) by Paul Hindemith illustrates a bimetric texture.

bimodality: The use of two modes at the same time. The modes may or may not have the same tonal center. See modality*. In example (a) below the two modes (Dorian and Phrygian) have the same tonal center—D. In example (b) the two modes (Mixolydian and Phrygian) have different tonal centers—G and D:

binary digit: See bit*.

binary input language: The representation of information by only two elements such as on or off, negative or positive charge, presence or absence of a hole in a card, etc. Binary input language is used to give instructions to electronic equipment including synthesizers* and computers*. See bit.*

bio-music: A term coined by ORCUS Research to denote studies using electronic systems that probe psychological/physiological states set in motion through aural and visual stimuli. Feedback* loops* are employed to study how the human organism organizes sensory stimuli in real-time* settings. The basic physiological parameters* studied include the use of galvanic skin response, electrocardiograms, electroencephalograms, electromylograms, blood pressure, and respiration rates.

bi-stable oscillator: See multi-vibrator*.

bit: An abbreviation for binary digit, the basic unit of information storage in a digital* computer. A bit consists of two possible states—1 and 0—which correspond to on and off, or impulse* and no impulse. The storage capacity of a computer is measured in bits (e.g., 2000 32-bit words).

bitonality: The simultaneous use of two different tonal centers or keys. The following example from *Song of Harvest* (*Forty-four Violin Duets* [1931]) by Béla Bartók is a clear illustration of bitonality.

black sound: This term is sometimes used to denote silence. It is the opposite of electronic white* sound in which all frequencies* are present.

block chords: Dense chords that usually move in parallel motion. Examples may be found in the piano music of Claude Debussy (e.g., *La Cathédrale engloutie* [1910]) or in the jazz* piano style of George Shearing.

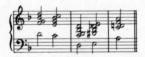

bluegrass: Country music as played on unamplified instruments such as banjo, mandolin, fiddle, and guitar. Bluegrass style involves polyphonic ensemble work much like that found in New* Orleans style jazz with many breaks and solos. Typically, each performer has a specific role to play. The guitar, bass and fiddle function as background instruments while the mandolin and five-string banjo are usually used for lead work. Some prominent bluegrass groups were Bill Monroe and his Bluegrass Boys of the 1930's and 1940's and the Foggy Mountain Boys of the 1950's and 1960's.

blue noise: A pitchless, non-repetitive

signal* containing all audible frequencies* with an increase in relative amplitude* of the higher frequencies. See white* noise, pink* noise.

blue note: A pitch of deliberate uncertain intonation in jazz*, often intended to be a compromise between major and minor when analyzed chordally or linearly. The third and seventh are the scale degrees most commonly adjusted to impart a blue quality. The fifth and sixth may also be treated as blue notes.

blues: 1. A song form stemming from the black slave culture in the United States, usually associated with melancholy, unrequited love, and sexuality. The blues is generally considered to be derived from a combination of spirituals* and European hymns, and in its earliest form it was closer to a type of speech-song rather than a song in the traditional sense. Early blues songs utilized an eight bar pattern based on I, IV, and V rather than the twelve bar pattern that developed later. Marshall Stearns has pointed out that many blues forms involve a three-part stanza. The first two lines are the same, and the third delivers the completion of the idea (A A B). 2. A synonym for a composition based on a blues* progression.

blues progression: A twelve measure sequence of basic chord changes* in jazz* based on the I, IV, and V chords. The number of chords employed may vary from three to twenty or more, depending upon the tune on which the blues progression is based and the particular genre of jazz (rhythm* and blues, progressive* jazz, dixieland*, etc.). The following examples represent 1. the most basic blues progression, and 2. a more complicated set of chord changes around the basic framework of I, IV, and V.

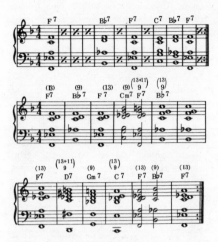

blues scale: A scale common to jazz*. Different chords may be chosen to harmonize the various scale degrees. Jazz players will usually select but a few of these tones as the primary basis for improvisation on a given tune.

BMI: Abbreviation for Broadcast* Music Incorporated.

Bode melochord: A monophonic* electronic sound generating instrument developed by H. Bode in the early 1950's. It has two independent keyboards and various other controls to alter pitch, duration, intensity, timbre*, and envelope*. The Bode melochord was used principally in the electronic* music studio of Radio* Cologne as both a sound synthesizer* for electronic composition and a performing instrument.

boo: See bamboo* marimba.

boobams: A bank of resonating bongo drums fastened together according to pitch differences suitable for rapid melodic passages. The sound of these drums is hollow and resonant, and the player usually employs wooden beaters. The most typical range for boobams is two chromatic octaves.

boogaloo: A kind of double-time* samba* that originated in New Orleans during the 1960's. The basic rhythm of the boogaloo is as follows:

boogie-woogie: An echoic term, suggesting the ostinato* bass pattern that characterizes this type of jazz*. Boogie-woogie pieces usually are modeled on a basic blues* progression in 4/4 meter. Important boogie-woogie pianists include Jimmy Yancey, Albert Ammons, Pine Top Smith, and Meade Lux Lewis. Two common boogie-woogie bass patterns appear below:

Book of Changes: See *I Ching**.

bonang panembung: Gong kettles found in Javanese gamelan* music.

bop: A term supposedly coined from the nonsense lyric "hey-ba-ba-re-bop" from the song of the same name composed by Lionel Hampton in 1945. The term is descriptive of a jazz style that extended from the early 1940's to the early 1950's. Stylistically, bop was introverted ("cool"), polyphonically inclined, and harmonically exploratory, depending heavily upon extended chords of the ninth*, eleventh*, and thirteenth*. Phrase structure was much more irregular than that of the swing music that preceded it, and there was extensive use of double-time* passages, unusual melodic intervals (particularly the diminished fifth), passing notes, and passing chords. Important musicians in the bop movement include Kenny Clarke, Miles Davis, Charlie Parker, Dizzy Gillespie, Buddy De-Franco, Benny Harris, Oscar Petti-ford, and Howard McGhee. See cool* jazz and flatted* fifth.

bossa nova: Jazz-influenced music from Brazil, developed from the samba*. The style is moody, nostalgic, subtle, and relaxed. The Brazilian composer Joao Gilberto is generally regarded as the father of the bossa nova. Other important musicians include Antonio Carlos Jobin, Astrud Gilberto, Luiz Bonfa, and the American jazz* saxophonist Stan Getz. The tune *Desafinado* is a good example of this style. The motion picture *Black Orpheus* was instrumental in generating enthusiasm for the bossa nova in the United States in the early 1960's. A typical bossa nova rhythmic pattern is indicated below.

boxes: The squares in graph* notation in which musical instructions are given.

brake drum: An automobile part with a clear, bell-like tone, usually struck with marimba mallets or metal mallets. It is possible to tune a brake drum to a specific pitch by the use of a grinding wheel.

break: A temporary stop in a jazz* piece while a soloist fills in a brief riff* or tiny solo before the ensemble work resumes.

Brechung: The arpeggiation of a chord in Schenkerian* analysis.

bridge: In popular and jazz* music the bridge is the B part of the ternary ABA structure. Generally the bridge* (also called release) is of lesser character than the surrounding A parts, although there are numerous exceptions. The typical AABA structure encompasses thirty-two measures. A is stated

three times, surrounding the bridge of eight measures. See chorus* and standards*.

Broadcast Music Incorporated: This organization, which licenses performing rights for its member composers and publishers, came into existence in 1940 after a dispute with ASCAP* when the contract between ASCAP and various radio stations expired. ASCAP demanded significantly higher payments from the stations under a new contract, with the result that BMI was formed as a rival organization. Many young songwriters joined BMI during the 1940's and 1950's, as ASCAP enforced very rigorous qualifications for membership. BMI is particularly active in rock* and roll and country* and western music as well as serious music.

bruitism: A movement connected with the Italian futurists* that saw musical possibilities inherent in noise. In 1913 a bruitist manifesto distinguished six families of noise. While no significant musical compositions evolved out of this movement, it is important as a forerunner of electronic* music and musique* concrète. See futurism*.

BTL: An abbreviation for Bell Telephone Laboratories (later shortened to Bell* Laboratories).

BTL system: A costly, high-speed method of computer* music generation devised by M. V. Mathews of the Bell* Laboratories that allows the generation of any mathematically describable sound with a fidelity similar to that achieved in modern recordings.

Buchla synthesizer: An electronic music synthesizer*, similar to the Moog*. Control on the Buchla synthesizer is accomplished by use of capacitive switches instead of by a keyboard as in the Moog. The Buchla also makes use of a sequencer*.

bucket notes: A term employed by composer, author, and teacher Vincent Persichetti to refer to notes in serial* music that are deleted from their natural order for a certain time span and then sprayed out at the end.

buffer: A unit of computer* equipment or circuitry used for the temporary storage and later transmission of data between two processing units.

buffer memory: See buffer*.

buffer storage: See buffer*.

building: In film* music this term is used to indicate the process of preparing a number of sound* tracks for dubbing*.

bulk eraser: An electrical device used to clear impulses* from magnetic* tape.

bull-roarer: A long slender piece of wood, usually attached to a string that produces a whipping or roaring sound as it is whirled over the head.

byte: A sequence of bits* that is processed as a unit in a computer*.

C

cacophony: Discordant, dissonant, or harsh sounds.

cakewalk: A dance developed in the late 1880's by American Negroes in which the couple exhibiting the most fancy or intricate stepwork would receive cakes as prize. The dance itself was much like a promenade or march. The black violinist, conductor, and composer, Will Marion Cook, presented *Clorindy, the Origin of the Cakewalk* on Broadway in 1899. The cakewalk quickly became a national craze after the presentation of this show.

CALCOMP: A computer* output* system capable of printing a selected set of symbols (triangles, lines, circles, etc.). CALCOMP has been used to plot a type of musical score on transparent paper.

cancrizans: See retrograde*.

capacitor: A device used in an electronic circuit* to store energy, block the flow of direct current,* and permit the flow of alternating current.

card punch: See key* punch.

cartridge: The removable section at the end of the tone arm of a record player which contains an electronic mechanism capable of transforming mechanical motion into electrical current. See tape* cartridge.

cassette: A plastic container for a length of ⅛ inch wide magnetic* tape designed to make manual threading unnecessary. The tape in a cassette runs back and forth between two rolls, automatically stopping at either extreme. See tape* cartridge.

Castor and Pollux: See harmonic* canon II.

cell: See basic* cell.

centric priority: The use of a given tone as the point of gravity in a composition without the more elaborate superstructure of tonality. Hence, a work or a passage of a work may center around a tone such as F♯ or D♭ without creating either a major/minor context or the chordal relationships found in tonal schemes. See polarity*.

cha-cha: An echoic term derived from the musical accompaniment of a Latin American dance popular during the 1950's. The cha-cha is similar to the mambo*. It relies upon the background rhythmic scheme illustrated below.

chance music: Music which relies on the element of randomness in its compositional processes and/or performance. See aleatory*, chance* operations.

chance operations: 1. The tossing of coins, rolling of dice, or other random processes used in the selection and ordering of musical material. **2.** Free or controlled improvisatory decisions made by the performer at the time of performance.

changes: Chord progressions in jazz*.

channel: A complete or partial pathway of electronic circuitry used in the reproduction of a sound. See track*, magnetic* tape, tape* recorder.

charleston: A type of dance popular during the 1920's, named for Charleston, South Carolina. The metric emphasis of the charleston is derived from the word itself:

charles - ton, charles - ton.

The dance was performed using rapid steps with an occasional kick done in place. It was first introduced to the public at large in 1923 by Cecil Mack and Jimmy Johnson as part of a Negro revue. It became a ballroom dance during the late 1920's.

chart: An arrangement* for a jazz* ensemble, particularly a big band*.

Chicago style: As the mainstream of jazz* moved from New Orleans to Chicago during the 1920's the earlier New* Orleans style underwent changes of great significance and became known as the Chicago style. Individual virtuosity as shown through solo work became more important, melodic invention became more complex, and the "hot" style of playing as demonstrated by Louis Armstrong became the new ideal. The impact of Louis Armstrong on other musicians cannot be underestimated, even though they may not have been trumpeters. Armstrong's characteristic vibrato, shake, and short but potent jazz phrases were imitated by musicians such as Earl Hines (piano), Coleman Hawkins (tenor saxophone), and Jimmy Harrison (trombone). At this juncture many white musicians such as Bix

Beiderbeck, Jimmy McPartland, Eddie Condon, Dave Tough, and Bud Freeman began to copy the innovations of the black musicians. The typical Chicago jazz ensemble contained four to seven men.

Chinese Book of Changes: See *I Ching**.

choir effect: Waveform* differences that create a tonal discrepancy when a group of voices or instruments is attempting to produce a unified sound.

chord cluster: The simultaneous sounding of two or more chords. See polychord*, tone-cluster*.

chord of addition: See added-note* chord.

chord of omission: An identifiable chord from which one or more structural elements has been removed. For example, a major triad or a seventh chord with no third:

chord of resonance: Composer Oliver Messiaen's term for a chord whose notes represent almost all the harmonics* above a given fundamental* that can be approximated in equal temperament.

chorus: 1. The primary thematic section of a popular song. See verse*, bridge*. 2. A jazz* improvisation* based on a given set of chords. See changes*, blues* progression.

chromatic cluster: A tone-cluster* consisting of minor seconds.

chromelodeon I: A keyboard instrument similar to a reed organ invented by composer Harry Partch that has six keyboard octaves with forty-three tones to the octave in just intonation. Three and one half octaves on the chromelodeon I are equivalent to one acoustic octave.

chronometer: A spring-driven or electronic timepiece of great accuracy often used to time chance* and film* music.

chronometric density: The relative frequency of rhythmic activity in a musical composition.

circuit: A path made up of various connections and conductors through which electrical current* flows.

circular permutation: A term from the Schillinger* system used to denote the displacing or rearranging of any group of pitches one step at a time until the original returns. For example, the motive C D A could be rearranged as D A C, A C D, followed by C D A again. See cyclical* permutation.

clangorous sounds: Strident, bell-like electronic sounds consisting of partials* that are not within the natural harmonic* series. Clangorous sounds are created by the intermodulation of two sine* waves in close proximity.

classical electronic music studio: A studio for the composition of electronic* music in which the primary consideration is tape* manipulation through speed variation, editing, reverberation*, loops, etc. Sound sources are usually the basic sine* wave, square* wave, and sawtooth* wave; and live sounds, rather than a synthesizer*.

click sheet: A guide for the film composer on which the numbered clicks of a click* track are coordinated with sound, dialogue, and events in the motion picture.

click track: A sound track containing small perforations that produce a clicking sound, used primarily by film composers and conductors to coordinate sound and visual events.

clipping: The level of power where distortion takes hold in an amplifier*.

closed loop: 1. An electronic circuit* that continuously feeds output* back to input* for comparison. 2. A computer*-program* with indefinitely repeated instructions. See loop*.

cloud-chamber bowls: An instrument invented by composer Harry Partch in 1950 that uses the inverted bottoms of twelve-gallon Pyrex carboys played on the edges with small soft mallets. The result in sound is a bell-like tone with at least one inharmonic partial*. The bowls are suspended on a rack seven feet long and six feet high.

clouded triads: See root* clouding.

cluster: See tone-cluster*.

cluster chord: See tone-cluster*.

cluster-rake: A nine-inch long wooden board with felt-tipped knobs developed by Carl Anders Zetterlund of Radio Sweden for use in playing tone-clusters on the organ.

COBOL: An acronym for Common Business Oriented Language which is a computer* programming* language designed primarily for data manipulation and processing. Some specialized programs* in music use COBOL as a means of presenting information to a computer.

cocktail drum: A versatile drum used primarily by jazz* musicians that can sound like a snare drum, bass drum, or tom-tom. This drum stands on metal legs with a foot pedal. Its portability and compactness make it desirable for the musician who must be able to set up and dismantle his equipment with ease. The drummer usually stands while playing this instrument.

code: A system of symbols for representing instructions or data in a computer*.

coded-performance music: Music produced by electronic devices and controlled by perforated paper tape* or punch* cards. Coded-performance music, which was brought to the attention of the public at the Paris

Exposition of 1929, stems from the player piano and organs which were in vogue in the first two decades of the twentieth century. In its earliest form, four monophonic* electronic oscillators* were controlled by a perforated paper roll device. In 1945, electronic equipment was developed to control the frequency*, intensity, duration, vibrato, and envelope*, of sound with punch cards.

coding: The translation of a program* into a form which a computer* can process directly (machine* language).

coins technique: The determination of various parameters* of a musical work through random selection by the tossing of a coin. See aleatory*, chance* operations, chance* music.

coin tossing: See coins* technique.

collage: In the visual arts this term signifies a work made by attaching cloth, paper, and other materials to a surface. A more general definition which would include its use in a musical context would be the superimposition of a number of disparate elements to form a unified whole. Examples of musical compositions containing collage are *Sinfonia* (1968) by Luciano Berio, *Gita* (1967) by R. Murray Schafer, and *Atmospheres* (1961) by György Ligeti. In these works many diverse sound events are overlapped and juxtaposed to create the total effect.

Cologne Electronic Studio: See Radio* Cologne.

Cologne Radio: See Radio* Cologne.

colored noise: Sound which results when a filter* is used to give emphasis to a particular band of the white* noise spectrum. See blue* noise, pink* noise.

color organ: An electronic device that translates audio* signals into visual light patterns of mixed colors. Color organs are frequently used in multimedia* art.

Columbia-Princeton Electronic Music Center: The first electronic* music studio to be established in the United States. It was founded in 1952 by Otto Luening and Vladimir Ussachevsky. Among the many other composers who have worked at Columbia are Milton Babbitt, Mario Davidovsky, and Mel Powell. See RCA* synthesizer, Radio* Cologne.

comatic scale: A scale consisting of fifty-three tones to the octave, proposed by the futurist* composers around 1912.

combination tone: A tone of different pitch that results from the simultaneous sounding of two loud tones of widely different frequencies*. See heterodyne*.

combinatoriality: A term originated by composer and theorist Milton Babbitt to describe a principle of set* (twelve-tone* row) construction first utilized by composer Arnold Schoenberg. In a combinatorial* set the first six notes (hexachord*) of the prime* can be "combined" with the first six notes of one or more of its transposed transformations* and there will be no duplication of pitches. The same relationship will apply to the second six notes of each of the two set-forms*. In both cases the twelve notes of the paired hexachords will all be different pitches. This property is particularly important in vertical set associations because it does not allow pitch repetitions in close proximity. There are three possibilities for combinatoriality: 1. between the prime and an inversion* (the second hexachord will be an inversion of the first); 2. between the prime and a retrograde-inversion* (each hexachord will be its own inversion); 3. between two transpositions (the second hexachord will be a transposition of the first). See all-combinatorial* set, semi-combinatorial* set. The following example of combinatoriality is from Arnold Schoenberg's *Fourth String Quartet* (1936):

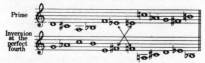

combinatorial set: See combinatoriality*, semi-combinatorial* set, all-combinatorial* set.

combine: A term used in film* music to indicate the process of reducing two or more sound* tracks to a single one by means of a mixer*.

combined meters: Two different meters that alternate back and forth in a composition. Usually a note value will be constant and equal between the two. The shift from one meter to the other will be characterized by the different stress pattern basic to each meter.

$$\begin{smallmatrix}3\\4\end{smallmatrix}\begin{smallmatrix}5\\8\end{smallmatrix} \; \text{♩. ♪♪} \; | \; \text{♫♫♫} \; | \; \text{♩. ♪♪} \; | \; \text{♫♫♫} | \quad \textit{etc.}$$

combo: A small jazz* or dance-band ensemble, consisting of three to six players, plus possibly a vocalist. Ensembles of seven or more performers are usually considered to constitute a band.

communication theory: See information* theory.

compiler: A computer* program* that converts other programs into machine* language.

comping: A jazz* term for the harmonic/rhythmic background supplied by the piano and guitar player in support of a soloist or an ensemble.

complex tone: A sound consisting of a number of pure pitches of varying frequency* and amplitude* that are called partials*. If these partials fall within the normal harmonic* series the result will be pitch. If they do not fall within the normal harmonic series the result will be noise or percussive sounds.

complementary sonorities: Composer-theorist Howard Hanson's term which refers to the fact that harmonic and melodic structures using some notes of the chromatic scale have a complementary sonority made up of the remaining notes. For example, the whole-tone* scale C, D, E, F♯, G♯, A♯ has a complementary scale of D♭, E♭, F, G, A, and B. The complementary scale has the same intervallic structure as the original. A major triad would have a complementary nine-tone scale which Hanson calls the "projection" of the major triad as it represents an expansion of the triad to a nine-tone order. These relationships, he claims, are crucial to the composer, as they allow him to expand tonal relationships with consistency.

composing-out: See compositional* unfolding.

compositional unfolding: The way in which a rudimentary musical structure comes to fulfillment through layers of complexity in an actual piece of music. The process is of more interest analytically than it is as an aid or guide to the composer. See Schenkerian* analysis.

computational music: Music that is arrived at through a primarily mathematical process.

computer: An electronic device consisting of from one to many separate pieces of equipment that is capable of receiving and processing data and storing instructions for controlling its own operation. See analog* computer, digital* computer.

computer music: 1. Music that is synthesized from information fed into and processed by a computer*. 2. Music in which the actual sounds are generated either within a computer or by equipment directly connected to a computer. Information for producing this music is fed into the computer by means of a program*. See digital* computer, analog* computer.

conditional jump: See conditional* transfer.

conditional transfer: The process by which a computer* skips certain instructions after predetermined criteria are satisfied.

conga: A dance in 4/4 meter of Latin American origin. The participants usually form a long, winding line holding on to one another. The dance had a brief vogue in the United States during the 1940's. A basic conga rhythm is seen in the example below.

constructivism: A movement in the visual arts that developed between 1918 and 1921 in the U.S.S.R. and had its origin in cubist* painting and the collages* of Pablo Picasso. Constructivism utilized materials such as glass, wood, paper, wire, metal, and string for a non-representational form of art in three dimensions. Primary constructionist artists included sculptors Naum Gabo, and Antoine Pevsner, and painter El Lissitsky. See abstract* art, suprematism*.

contact mike: A microphone* that is attached to a vibrating medium and transforms physical vibrations into electrical current*.

controlled improvisation: A process whereby the performer has the option of selecting specific motives, rhythms, or patterns which he then employs, either in the original form or modified, within a certain time span in a composition. Composers such as Lukas Foss, Gunther Schuller, Morton Feldman, Karlheinz Stockhausen and Harold Budd have used this technique extensively.

controller: An electronic device that exercises an influence over other electronic devices in a prescribed manner. See manual* controller, keyboard* controller, sequential* controller, linear* controller.

cool jazz: A term often applied to bop* and the progressive* jazz of the 1950's in which intellectualism and emotional restraint were paramount as opposed to the fervor of the earlier varieties of hot* jazz. The recordings made by the Modern Jazz Quartet in the mid-1950's are examples of cool jazz.

coordinome: A punched tape reading device developed by Stein G. Raustein and Emmanuel Ghent at New York University that translates basic signals* (perforations on tape) into audio* signals on magnetic* tape. The coordinome is so named because it has the function of coordinating live performers playing in different meters, different tempi. and/or different locations with tape* music.

corresponding segments: Groups of notes that occupy the same relative position in two different twelve-tone* rows or different forms of the same tone row. For example, the first hexachord* of one row-form and the first hexachord of another row-form as used by Arnold Schoenberg in *Concerto for Violin* (1936):

counterchord: A contrapuntal technique utilizing chords in separate streams or plateaus juxtaposed one against the other. Composer Henry Cowell sets forth this term in his book *New Music Resources* (1930). See bichord*.

country and western: A blend of popular song from the American southern and western regions. Country and western style is often terse to the point of being droll, sentimentally inclined, harmonically and rhythmically simple and straightforward, and usually sung in a style devoid of the kind of vibrato found in other popular music. The violin, string bass, guitar, and banjo form the instrumental nucleus of this style. Country (sometimes called "hillbilly") music has its roots in Elizabethan songs carried to this country by early settlers. It usually deals with subjects such as love or personal problems, whereas western music, as a style unto itself, tends to focus on subjects pertaining to nature and the out-of-doors. After World War II the two styles began to merge into one, and this new fusion spread to all parts of the country as a viable musical idiom.

coupling: 1. The transference of power from one electronic circuit* to another. 2. A term from the Schillinger* system used to denote a melodic line that has a parallel sequence added to it. For example, a melody in octaves would be diatonic coupling at the octave.

cps: Abbreviation for cycles* per second. See hertz*.

crooner: A singer of popular songs who utilizes a soft, soothing style of delivery. Some famous crooners include Rudy Vallee, Bing Crosby, Perry Como and Frank Sinatra.

cross-coupling: A technique used in electronic* music in which the output* of one channel* of a tape* recorder is fed into the input* of another channel. At the same time, the output of the second channel is fed back to the input of the first. This results in a modification of the attack* and decay* characteristics of the original sound.

cross-fade: A film-score technique in which two sound tracks are merged; one gradually fading out while the other fades in and becomes dominant.

cross meter: See polymeter*.

cross rhythm: Rhythmic patterns such as two notes against three, three against four, two against five, etc.

Sometimes the term is applied incorrectly to bi-metric* schemes such as 2/4 against 3/4. See polymeter*, polyrhythm*.

crosstalk: Signal* leakage between two adjacent channels* on magnetic* tape.

CSL system: A simple, computer-based music generation system intended to minimize cost by using a computer* of modest size and speed (i.e., 1/100 of the BTL* system) devised by the Coordinated Science Laboratory of the University of Illinois. See computer* music.

cubism: An early twentieth century movement in the plastic and graphic arts characterized by the representation of objects in terms of their geometric, linear, and spatial components. Basic to the concept of cubism was the idea that art should no longer imitate nature. Rather, it should contain the imposition upon nature of forms such as the cylinder, sphere, and cone as conceived in the mind of the artist. In this way objects could be viewed in terms of their component parts, and elements of what is depicted could be distorted in order to focus on particular component parts rather than on the whole. The cubists were also interested in the two-dimensional quality of the canvas, and eschewed the idea that a canvas should display three-dimensional orientation in order to imitate natural space. Georges Braque and Pablo Picasso are often credited as the originators of cubism. Other important cubists were Juan Gris, Marchel Duchamp, and Fernand Léger. Picasso's *Three Musicians* (1921) is a good example of a cubist work.

cut: A technique used in motion picture editing in which one segment of film is spliced directly to another, creating an immediate change of subject or view. Composers of film* music use cuts as important points of precise coordination between picture action and music.

cybernetics: The comparative study of human control functions (the nervous system) and mechanical-electrical communications systems such as telephone networks and computers*.

cycle: 1. One complete vibration or oscillation, usually expressed in units of time or hertz*. (For example, 440 cycles per second or 440 hertz.) 2. A circular pattern of instructions for a computer*.

cycles per second: See hertz*.

cyclic permutation: The alteration of a basic set* or twelve-tone* row which occurs when its interval structure is manipulated according to a controlling numerical sequence. See example under cyclic* transposition.

cyclic transposition: The transposition* of a twelve-tone* row or set* according to a previously established numerical sequence. For example, transposition down one half-step beginning on the second note, then down two half-steps beginning on the third note, etc.

D

dada: An art movement that grew out of the grief and nihilism following World War I in which traditional values were castigated and deemed worthless. Dada is a type of anti-art, and its practitioners delighted in shocking, boring, or antagonizing audiences. The movement is im-

portant philosophically in that it shows a disillusionment with the world, places nonsense on a level with profundity, and values incongruity and the hopelessness that many feel with regard to contemporary life. Some important dadaists include Marcel Duchamp, Giorgio de'Chirico, Marc Chagall, Salvador Dali, and the American painter Robert Rauschenberg. In music, John Cage and Morton Feldman are often identified with this school. Cage's *Theatre Piece* (1965) is a good example of a dadaist work. A man hangs upside down wrapped in a black plastic cocoon while a female cellist performs as she watches the composer place a cigar in and out of his mouth. At the same time, a tiny Japanese man waves a silken banner from atop a bamboo pole while oil drums are rolled down stairs, balloons are broken, buzzers are sounded, and electronic noises fill the air.

damping: The progressive reduction of energy within a vibrating system. See damping* factor.

damping factor: A scaled numerical indication of the ability of an amplifier* to drive a loudspeaker*.

DARMS: An acronym for Digital Alternate Representation of Music Symbols (also known as the Ford-Columbia representation), a computer* programming* language that was developed by Stefen Bauer-Mengelberg and others. DARMS can accurately encode both pitch and rhythm, and its creators are hopeful that it will be of future use in music printing by computer.

data card: See punch* card.

db: See decibel*.

DC: 1. An abbreviation for cancrizans* of the duration* series. 2. An abbreviation for direct current.

dead cue: A term used in film* music to indicate the precise place in a picture sequence that the composer intends to accent with music.

debug: The process of locating and removing mistakes in a computer* program* or malfunctions in a computer.

decad: A vertical* sonority consisting of ten different pitches.

decay: In electronic* music, decay refers to the amplitude* characteristics at the end of a sound.

decibel: A unit for measuring the loudness of sound. A change in intensity of one decibel is the smallest change ordinarily recognizable by the human ear. Decibel stands for one-tenth of a bel (from the name of Charles Graham Bell). The bel is the fundamental division of a logarithmic scale for expressing the ratio of two amounts of power. An increase of ten decibels means a tenfold increase in sound intensity; a twenty decibel rise, a hundredfold increase; and a thirty decibel rise, a thousandfold increase. The magnitude of the decibel approximates the following sound events: very soft violin (5-10 dbs), a busy street (50-90 dbs), a full symphony orchestra (80-90 dbs), and a loud rock* ensemble (130-140 dbs).

deci-talas: A table of Hindu rhythmic patterns that composer Oliver Messiaen has utilized in the composition of a number of works.

degenerate set: A twelve-tone* row that cannot be transformed into a set-complex* of forty-eight distinct forms through inversion*, retrograde*, retrograde-inversion*, and transposition*. Examples include some of Anton Webern's rows in which the prime* and the retrograde-inversion are identical.

Degausser: German for demagnetizer*.

delta wave: See triangular* wave.

demagnetizer: An electrical device used to remove accumulated magnetism from the tape* heads of a tape* recorder. Demagnetizing is warranted when a tape recorder is not producing high frequencies* with the fidelity it should, or when sounds are not as bright as they once were.

density: The relative complexity of a given musical layer or strata, which takes into account the number of notes occurring horizontally and vertically at a given point.

deranged set: A twelve-tone* row or segment of a row in which the original* order has been changed.

derivation technique: The generation of a twelve-tone* row (set*) through the transformation* of a three, four, or six note unit. The row in Anton Webern's *Concerto for Nine Instruments* (1935) illustrated below is arrived at through derivation technique. A three-note prime* is followed by its retrograde-inversion*, its retrograde*, and its inversion*:

derivation row: See derivation* technique.

derived set: See derivation* technique.

DI: An abbreviation for inversion* of the duration* series.

diad: See dyad*.

diamond marimba: An instrument built by composer Harry Partch in 1946 that measures forty inches in height and thirty-three inches in width. Thirty-six Brazilian rosewood and pernambuco blocks are mounted on foam rubber above resonators constructed of Brazilian bamboo. The instrument has a range of almost three octaves, and the blocks are arranged in diagonal rows to facilitate arpeggio-like chords played with a single sweep of the mallet.

DIC: An abbreviation for inverted cancrizans* of the duration* series.

digital computer: A calculating machine that solves problems and processes data in numerical or symbolic form. This is accomplished through an arithmetical process. See digital* tape, analog* computer, computer* music.

digital signal: A signal* consisting of simple magnetic pulses used to represent numbers, symbols or other information that can be expressed in digits.

digital tape: Magnetic* tape used to store information conveyed in a numerical sequence of impulses*.

digital to analog conversion: The changing of digital* signals (data in numerical or symbolic form) to analog* signals (data in varying voltage* form). This process is very important in electronic* music and computer* music. Information for the generation of sound can be fed into, and processed by, a computer in digital form and then converted to analog form for direct application to electronic equipment such as oscillators*, amplifiers, filters*, and entire synthesizers*.

digital to analog converter: An electronic computing device that accomplishes digital* to analog conversion.

diminution: A compositional technique in which the duration values of a group of notes are decreased by the same proportion. This is accomplished by deducting from the value of each note in the group the equivalent of ½, ¼, ⅛, etc., of its original value.

diodic texture: A type of dual linearity in music. Instead of having one prominent line supported by harmonic blocks (as in homophony) or two independent lines (as in polyphony), a diodic texture would have the second melody linked in harmonization with the first, as both parts move in basically consonant intervals, while each retains its individual integrity.

direct access: See random* access.

directive graphics: A type of notation (developed primarily for use in aleatoric* works) containing symbols for pitch, dynamics, and tempo that permit the performer a certain amount of freedom in his reaction to and interpretation of the score.

direct-wire recording: A tape made directly from an electronic sound source such as a phonograph, radio, another tape* recorder, an electronic* music synthesizer*, or an electronic piano. One patch* cord is plugged into an output* jack* of the sound source while the other is plugged into the auxiliary input* of the receiving tape recorder in order to make the recording.

disk file: A rotating disk with magnetic coating used for the storage of information in a computer* network.

disk pack: A set of disk* files that can be moved in and out of a computer's* disk* storage as a unit.

disk storage: The section of a computer* network where information is stored on disk* files.

dismemberment: The omission or reordering of chords within a harmonic progression.

dissonant counterpoint: The unrestricted use of dissonances (seconds, sevenths, augmented and diminished intervals) to create a musical texture in which individual lines are strongly independent.

distortion: Undesirable changes in the

frequency* and amplitude* of a waveform* that occur between the input* and output* phases of an electronic system.

divisionism: See pointillism*.

divisive meter: Meter in which certain substructural rhythms become regular enough to create an internal metric structure within the context of the stated meter. For example, in a triple meter such as 3/4, constant subdivision of the basic quarter note units into sixteenth notes would create a substructural metric framework that could operate simultaneously within the larger meter implied by one entire measure of three quarter-notes.

dixieland: A type of jazz* performed by a small combo* which typically includes trumpet, trombone, clarinet, piano, string bass, and banjo. The harmonic style employs basic triads and seventh chords, often linking them in chains of secondary dominant progressions. Dixieland stems from the earliest jazz influences, such as march music and ragtime*, found in New Orleans at the turn of the century. The word itself supposedly stems from the fact that in New Orleans a ten-dollar bill with "dix" printed on it came to mean Dixie, or New Orleans. The group known as the Original Dixieland Jazz Band (1912), which was composed entirely of white musicians, is considered to be the first major dixieland ensemble. A tune such as *Muskrat Ramble* is a good example of dixieland style.

doad: See dyad*.

dodecaphonic: Pertaining to twelve-tone* technique.

dodecaphony: See twelve-tone* technique.

dodecuple scale: A consecutive ordering of the twelve different notes within an octave with the intention of treating all twelve as equally im-

portant rather than as embellishments of a diatonic scale.

doink: An upward bending and tapering off of a pitch in jazz*. This effect may be indicated in either of the two ways below:

Dolby noise reduction system: An acoustical invention devised by the English engineer Ray Dolby that is employed in the recording studio to eliminate tape* hiss commonly found during the quieter moments of a recording. See tape* recording.

Doppler effect: The frequency* change of a sound wave caused by a continuous decreasing or increasing of the distance between the source and the listener. As the distance decreases the frequency will be higher than the source; as the distance increases it will be lower.

double harmonic scale: A synthetic° scale in which both tetrachords* have the same structure as the upper tetrachord of the harmonic minor scale.

double time: A device common to jazz* in which the performer plays twice as fast within a given metric framework. The impression created is one of feeling two measures within the context of one. For example, in a 4/4 meter the performer may string out long runs of eighth notes or sixteenth notes which creates the feeling of moving twice as fast as the prevailing pulse.

double tracking: In film* music this term is used to indicate the simultaneous utilization of two or more complete music tracks*.

doubling: Distortion heard in a loudspeaker* system when harmonics* of bass tones are inadvertently produced.

drift: A gradual, undesired change in some characteristic of an electronic circuit* usually brought about by equipment malfunction. In electronic* music, drift is usually identified with oscillator* frequency*.

drop out: A momentary distortion or change in the amplitude* of a signal* produced by an imperfection in the metallic-oxide coating of magnetic* tape or film.

DS: An abbreviation for duration* series.

dual modality: A technique in which two different modes with the same tonic operate simultaneously in a work. The term also is used occasionally as a synonym for bitonality*.

dual ring modulator: A two-channel version of the ring* modulator in which both channels* utilize a common power supply. The dual ring modulator is frequently used as a sound modifier in electronic* music studios.

dual trigger delay: Two trigger* delay units that are mounted on the same chassis and interconnected.

dub: A reproduced copy of recorded audio or visual information from tape*, film, or phonograph record.

dubbing: The process of copying recorded audio or visual information from tapes*, films, or phonograph records.

dub-down: A process used in electronic* music composition whereby two or more channels of recorded audio* material are combined into a single channel by means of a mixer*.

dulcitone: A keyboard percussion instrument with a subtle bell-like tone similar to the celeste. Steel tuning forks are struck by hammers connected to dampers operated by a foot pedal. The instrument differs from the celeste primarily in that it has a more sustained tone and a

greater timbral depth. It is sometimes used in situations requiring a celeste. Its range is four octaves, starting from C below middle C. D'Indy used the dulcitone in his orchestral work *Chant de La Cloche* (1886).

dummy: A 35MM playback* machine that is electronically synchronized with a motion picture projector. A number of dummies can be utilized at one time through a mixer* allowing for the coordination of various sound* tracks and picture action.

duodecad: A vertical* sonority consisting of twelve different pitches.

duodecophony: See twelve-tone* technique.

duodecuple scale: See dodecuple* scale.

duration registration: See duration* series.

duration scale: An ordering of a number of note values (usually twelve) in which each successive value increases in duration by a specified amount. See duration* series.

duration series: An ordering of the note values of a duration* scale that is similar in principle to the ordering of pitches in a twelve-tone* row.

duration set: See duration* series.

dyad: A vertical* sonority consisting of two different pitches.

dynamic envelope control: See envelope* generator.

dynamophone: See telharmonium*.

dynaphone: 1. Another name for tel-harmonium*. 2. An electronic musical instrument invented by René Bertrand capable of producing all audible pitches with various timbres. Only single tones, fifths, and octaves were possible on a single instrument but several instruments were often combined in performance to widen the range of contrapuntal and harmonic possibilities. Among the early compositions that employed the dynaphone was Honegger's ballet, *Rose de Métal* (1928).

E

earphones: See headphones*.

East Coast jazz: A vague term used to distinguish jazz of the 1950's as performed in the New York area from West* Coast jazz in California. East Coast jazz focused more on a revival of the blues* in a modern context and favored a "funky" sound as opposed to the smoother, more contrapuntal and intellectual sound of West Coast jazz. Some prominent musicians identified with East Coast jazz are Donald Byrd, Kenny Dorham, and Art Farmer.

echo: The replication of a sound which occurs when the original wave strikes a reflective surface. The amplitude* of the echo is usually less than the amplitude of the original sound. See reverberation*.

Eccles-Jordan trigger: See flip-flop*.

echo chamber: An enclosed space that has a very high resonance factor and reverberation* capacity.

echo unit: See reverberation* unit.

eight-track cartridge tape recorder: A two-channel (stereo*) tape* recorder or playback* unit in which each channel* is ⅛ the width of a quarter-inch tape. In order to take advantage of all eight tracks* the channels are switched internally by manipulating the tape* heads. This

tape recorder is used primarily in automobile sound systems.

eight-track recording: See multiple-track* recording.

eight-track tape recorder: A tape* recorder that uses eight separate channels* simultaneously in the recording and playback* processes. See multiple-track* tape recording.

electric bass: A bass instrument used by jazz* and rock* groups that looks like a large guitar. The sound of the electric bass is amplified electronically and volume is easily controlled. Many jazz and rock bassists use both the standard string bass and the electric bass.

electric music: An experimental kind of electronic* music composition in which the actual sound of high voltage* electricity is the basic source material rather than signals* produced by oscillators* or other sound generators.

electro-acoustics: The science of combining electrical and acoustical processes and devices, which results in such items as microphones* and loudspeakers*.

ElectroComp synthesizer: A small portable electronic* music synthesizer* produced by Electronic Music Laboratories, Inc. The basic unit may be expanded by the addition of a manual* controller and a keyboard* controller. The synthesizer provides for the basic electronic sound sources as well as means to modify them.

electronic monochord: An electronic* musical instrument developed from the trautonium* of the late 1920's which can be used either as a performance instrument or to synthesize sounds for electronic* music composition. It has a variable frequency* range controlled by two manuals with five keys over each octave in a similar pattern to the black keys of a standard piano keyboard. The keys are tuned to whatever pitches are required in the composition. The basic waveform* in the electronic monochord is saw-tooth*. Formant* filters are used to vary timbre*.

electronic music: Music that is wholly or partially the result of the electronic generation, processing, and reproduction of sound. Electronic music was fostered by the development of the tape* recorder, culminating around 1950. The first studio for the production of electronic music was established at Radio* Cologne in 1951 under the direction of Herbert Eimert. Important composers who began work at Cologne were Eimert, Robert Beyer, and Karlheinz Stockhausen. Shortly thereafter Luciano Berio and Bruno Maderna began electronic music composition at a new Italian Radio studio in Milan. Pioneering work in electronic music was done in the United States by Otto Luening and Vladimir Ussachevsky, who later became directors of the important Columbia-Princeton* Electronic Music Center. Early electronic music was created mainly through various methods of tape* manipulation. The development of the synthesizer* made the composition of electronic music much more flexible and accessible by rendering many manual operations unnecessary. Recent experimental activity in electronic music has centered around the computer*. See tape* recorder music, musique* concrète, computer* music, electronic* musical instrument.

electronic musical instrument: Any musical instrument whose sound is wholly or partially produced by electronic means. Early experimentation in the development of electronic musical instruments was undertaken by Thaddeus Cahill before the turn of the century. In the 1920's and 1930's Leon Theremin, a Russian, invented a number of musical instruments whose sounds were produced elec-

tronically. Other inventors active at this time were Jörg Mager and Friedrich Trautwein in Germany, Maurice Martenot in France, and Laurens Hammond in the United States. The work of these early experimenters paved the way for electronic* music and the synthesizer*. See appendix under electronic* musical instruments for a listing of those included in this volume.

electronic music studio: A place where electronic* music is created. Size, scope, and equipment vary considerably from studio to studio. Basic equipment falls into three categories: 1. sound sources (oscillators*, white* noise generators, etc.); 2. sound modifiers* (filters*, envelope* generators, amplifiers*, etc.); 3. tape* recorders. See classical* electronic music studio and appendix under electronic music.

electronic sackbut: A monophonic* electronic* musical instrument developed by Canadian radio engineer Hugh LeCaine between 1945 and 1948. Despite the name, which was assigned so that it would not be confused with any existing instruments, the electronic sackbut functions with a keyboard. The keys are tuned to the equal-tempered scale but horizontal pressure on a key will vary the pitch. Vertical pressure on a key controls loudness, attack*, and decay*. Timbre* is controlled by the left hand and can be changed during the attack. Basic waveform* can be varied by turning a knob with the index finger. Two formant* controls are manipulated by the thumb, and three other fingers control departure of the waveform from periodicity*.

electrophonic music: See electronic* music.

electrosonic music: See electronic* music.

electrosonics: The science of producing sounds electronically, which includes noise, music, sonic experiments, etc.

elekronische musik: German for electronic* music.

elektrophon: An early electronic* musical instrument developed by Jörg Mager. The elektrophon was developed in Berlin in 1924, and was a descendent of an earlier machine called the sphärophon*.

eleventh chord: A tertian* sonority with a basic structure consisting of six different notes. An eleventh chord can be viewed as a combination of two triads, one placed over the other with the interval of a third between. Depending on the exact intervals present it may or may not have a dominant function. Example (a) below illustrates an eleventh chord viewed as a combination of a C major triad and a B diminished triad. Example (b) illustrates an eleventh chord that could function as a dominant.

EMAMu: A group of electronic engineers, psychologists, philosophers, mathematicians, and musicians organized by the composer Iannis Xenakis in Paris to study the development and production of automated music through philosophic, aesthetic, and causal determinants.

emicon: A monophonic* electronic* musical instrument developed in the United States around 1930 by N. Langer and J. Halmagyi which was operated by a keyboard of thirty-two notes.

enigmatic scale: A synthetic* scale first used by Verdi in *Ave Maria* (1898) consisting of seven notes arranged in the following interval pattern:

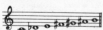

entropy: 1. A measure of the degree of disorder or randomness in a computer* or other communications system. **2.** A static or inactive condition.

envelope: The amplitude* curve of a sound from its beginning to its end consisting of three stages: **1.** rise* time — the time needed for the sound to reach its maximum amplitude; **2.** steady-state* — the time the maximum amplitude continues; **3.** decay* — the time needed for the amplitude to decrease from maximum level to inaudibility.

envelope follower: An electronic device that generates a voltage* reflecting the rise* time, steady* state, and decay characteristics of a signal* applied to it. See envelope*, envelope* generator.

envelope generator: An electronic device which, when coupled with an amplifier*, can control the rise* time, steady-state*, and decay* of a sound in a precise and variable manner. See envelope*.

environmental art: The use of objects and sounds from the environment for artistic creations. For example, a sculptor might choose rusted car bodies or melted down beer bottles for his creations, while a musician might employ doorbells or empty garbage cans as musical instruments.

eoliphone: See wind* machine.

equalizer: A network of electronic components that alters the response of a transmission circuit in a specified way. Equalizers are used to correct undesirable frequency* characteristics.

equiton: A system of music notation invented by Rodney Fawcett and further developed by Erhard Karkoschka. One staff line per octave is used along with unstemmed white or black note heads. Duration is indicated by the relative horizontal spacing of the notes and by extension lines. The use of accidental signs is entirely eliminated.

erase head: A device on a tape* recorder that breaks down magnetic patterns on tape, returning the oxide particles to a random state of magnetism. An erase head is used to remove previous recordings from magnetic* tape.

escaped chord: The use of a chord alien to the key in which it is found. The escaped chord is so-called because it is usually not prepared or resolved in the traditional manner, and it most often occurs on a weak beat.

etherophone: An early electronic* musical instrument developed in Russia around 1920 by Leon Theremin (also called the thereminovox). The etherophone consists of a small box housing the electronic components with a metal rod extending from it. The proximity of the player's hand to the rod controls the pitch. The other hand is used to terminate sounds by means of a switch if a continuous tone with glissando to the next pitch is not desired. Loudness is controlled by a foot pedal. A more sophisticated electronic musical instrument, the theremin*, was developed from the etherophone.

evaporation: The resolution of a dissonant tone by skipping to another member of the same chord.

event: A specific musical detail such as a chord, a theme, a figure, etc. The term also is sometimes used as a synonym for happening*.

exact notation: The standard notational system in use prior to the twentieth century as opposed to graphic* notation, indicative* notation, frame* notation, etc.

exclusion filter: See band-elimination* filter.

exoticism: Exoticism does not denote a specific movement in art or music, but refers (in the case of music) to the interest European and American composers of the twentieth century have shown in the music of non-Western cultures and the effect it

has had upon their musical thinking. John Cage, for example, was influenced by the music of the Far East as seen in his *Music of Changes* (1952). Also, the use of devices and sounds from Indian music can be found in many avant-garde* and rock* scores.

expanded tonality: Music in which traditional progressions and cadences are clouded and extended by the use of chromatic passing chords, harmonic deviations, and free key relationships. Richard Strauss' *Elektra* and *Salome* are works in this style.

experimental music: See avant-garde*.

expressionism: Expressionism in art seeks to explore the inner consciousness. The irrational, the primitive, and the mysterious are important, and above all, the artist must strive to express his personal viewpoint or feelings. The movement started with such painters as Klee, Kandinsky, and Kokoschka. Their distorted hallucinations on canvas with the ever-present aura of the romantic, sensual, and macabre were paralleled in the music of such composers as Richard Strauss, Arnold Schoenberg, and Alban Berg. As these composers forged a new musical language that "distorted" melody and harmony through the use of wide leaps, extreme registers, and new textures the very foundation of music in the traditional sense was shaken. A work like Schoenberg's *Pierrot Lunaire* (1912), half sung, half spoken, with its sudden shifts between the sordid and romantic is a true manifestation of the expressionistic spirit in music. Other composers who were influenced by expressionism include Anton Webern, Ernst Krenek, and Paul Hindemith.

eye music: A term often applied to contemporary scores that contain visual patterns, graphic symbols, or other special and unusual methods of notation designed to attract the eye with new and novel complexes of design. *Circles* (1960), by Luciano Berio and *New York Skyline* (1940) by Heitor Villa-Lobos would be scores of this type. See millimetration*.

F

facade design: See arch* form.

falsetto break: A type of yell executed loudly in a falsetto voice common to jazz*. It is derived from the "field holler" of the blacks during the days of slavery.

falsonance: Theorist Joseph Yasser's term for an interval or harmonic combination that, regardless of its intrinsic harmoniousness or inharmoniousness, is alien to a given scale. Hence, intervals not found in a given tonal system are not regarded as either consonances or dissonances. For example, the acoustically pure major third (5:4) which is a consonance in the diatonic system would be labeled a falsonance in Yasser's infra-diatonic* scale, because the only major third in the just intonation of this scale would be F-A, which is a dissonance.

fauvism: A term stemming from the French "les fauves" or "wild beasts" which was applied to a group of revolutionary painters of the early 20th century because of their use of strident color and violent distortions of form. This pre-cubist* art movement rejected impressionism* and was concerned with the inner qualities of subjects rather than their appearance in nature. Matisse was the leader of the loose-knit group whose paintings were in this style. The expressionists* Maurice de Vlaminck and Andre Derain, much influenced by Vincent Van Gogh in their use of color for emotional and symbolic power, were an important part of the fauvist movement. Other artists were Georges Rouault and Albert Marquet. Musical works by such composers as Edgar Varèse and Charles Ives paralleled the creative endeavors of the fauvists.

feedback: 1. The returning of a portion of the output* of an electronic circuit* or device back to its input*. 2. The return of information concerning the condition under control in a computer* process.

Fernhören: A term from Schenkerian* analysis that may be translated as "distance-hearing". It connotes the ability of the listener to perceive the fundamental structure or Ursatz* of a composition.

fiber sculpture: A type of textile art using silk, wool, horsehair, rope, linen, or synthetic fibers which are woven, knitted, crocheted, or twisted into art constructions. Most often the finished product is gigantic in size as in Neda Al-Hilali's sixteen-foot wall hanging of knotted wool, rayon, and nylon fibers. Works in this form are hung against the wall, suspended from the ceiling, or flung across the floor. Fiber sculpture attempts to create three-dimensional forms that surround and captivate the viewer. Important artists include Lenore Tawney, Olga de Amaral, Claire Zeisler, Magdalena Abakanowicz, and Francoise Grossen.

Fibonacci sequence: A series of numbers that reads 1, 1, 2, 3, 5, 8, 13, 21, 34, 55, 89 . . . etc. Each number, after the second, is the sum of the two previous numbers. This sequence was discovered by the thirteenth century Italian mathematician Leonardo Fibonacci. Ernö Lendvai, in his book, *Béla Bartók, an Analysis of His Music*, claims that Bartók used the Fibonacci sequence in setting proportions of length between and within movements and in determining chordal structures, scales, and melodic motifs. For example, Lendvai states that in the fugue from the first movement of *Music for Strings, Percussion, and Celesta* that the 89 bars of the movement are divided into sections of 55 and 34 bars. This form further subdivides in the first 55 measures as a grouping of 34+12 while the latter 34 measures divides into a grouping of 13+21.

fifteenth chord: A tertian* sonority with a basic structure consisting of eight different notes. It can be viewed as a combination of two seventh chords, one placed over the other, with the interval of a third between. The interval of the fifteenth above the root must be augmented or a thirteenth* chord with an octave doubling will result.

film music: Music that is written to enhance a motion picture or television production.

film phonograph: An electronic device used to reproduce the sounds recorded on photographic or magnetic* tape.

film recorder: An electronic device that records sound on photographic or magnetic* tape.

filter: An electronic device that transmits desired frequencies* while attenuating* others.

finger drumming: Tapping the fingers on the body of an instrument, a technique common in avant-garde* scores.

first order set: A term originated by composer and theorist Milton Babbitt to designate a source* set that creates combinatorial* relationships at only one level of transposition. See combinatoriality*.

fixed band-pass filter: A band-pass* filter in which the specified limits for transmission and attenuation are nonadjustable.

fixed filter bank: A group of fixed filter units (usually fixed* band-pass filters) housed within a single chassis.

flatted fifth: The lowered fifth scale degree in a harmonic or melodic structure, especially as used in jazz*. To be precise, the lowered quality of the note should indicate a basically downward melodic inflection, but, in practice, the flatted fifth is often used as an augmented fourth with an intended upward resolution. See bop*.

Fletcher-Munson curve: A curve which indicates deviations in the frequency* response of the ear at differing loudness levels. At lower loudness levels the ear tends to respond less efficiently to extreme high or low frequencies.

flexatone: A kind of musical saw with a high-pitched, biting sound. The pitch range of the instrument is wide, and it has a vibrating sound especially effective when performing glissandi. The main components of the flexatone are a thin triangular steel blade fitted into a metal frame with a handle at one end. Curved steel strings are fastened to the sides of the blade with a softwood ball on each end. The softwood balls strike the blade when the handle is shaken, producing its characteristic tremolo effect. Arnold Schoenberg, in his *Variations for Orchestra* (1928) wrote a part for the flexatone requiring exact pitch, but more often this is considered impractical and it is treated as a nonpitched instrument. Other composers who have written for the flexatone include Toshiro Mayuzumi in his *Mikrokosmos* (1957), and Mauricio Kagel in *Match für 3 Spieler* (1969).

flip-flop: A circuit* used in computers* and synthesizers* which has two stable states. An input* pulse of short duration causes a change of state. The new state then holds until another pulse causes a switch back to the first state.

flow chart: A graphic representation of the procedures and operations necessary to define, analyze, and solve a problem. This term is often used in connection with computers*.

flutter tongue: A type of articulation used on wind instruments (particularly flute, piccolo, and brass) in which the player rolls his tongue as though saying "drrr". The result is a kind of dry and rapid tremolo on a single pitch. Richard Strauss was among the first to employ the technique in Don Quixote (1898). Since that time it has found great favor with many composers.

flux: The metallic-oxide coating on magnetic* tape.

Fluxus: A group of New York-based composers, poets, and artists who banded together in the 1960's because of their shared concern with boredom, danger, and environmentalism as artistic concepts. Among the people who have been associated with Fluxus are Eric Anderson, George Brecht, Dick Higgins, Nam June Paik, Thomas Schmit, Jackson Mac Low, and La Monte Young.

FM: See frequency* modulation.

Ford-Columbia representation: See DARMS*.

foreground: A term set forth by the theorist Heinrich Schenker to denote the musical events* of a work most readily perceived by the listener. In this context the foreground would include surface structure such as themes, texture, motives, and primary structural divisions. See background*, middleground*, Ursatz*, Urlinie*, Schenkerian* analysis.

formalism: A derogatory term applied to the works of composers in the U.S.S.R. such as Prokofiev, Shostakovich, and Miaskovsky by govern-ment spokesmen in 1948. Formalism in music was defined as encompassing a lack of substance, content, form, and emotional values that interfered with the ability of the music to penetrate the human consciousness in a direct and convincing manner.

formant: A specific resonant frequency* (or frequencies) present in the harmonic* spectrum of a musical instrument which influences the tone color or timbre* of the sound through its interaction with the harmonic* series of the note being played.

formant filter: An electronic filter* that emphasizes a particular narrow band* of frequencies*. Formant filters are used to alter the timbre* of generated waveforms*.

formant spectrum: The formant* frequencies* present in any sound-generating instrument.

FORTRAN: A computer* programming* language which allows the programmer to state in relatively simple terms the procedure to be carried out by the computer. The instructions in FORTRAN are then translated into machine* language at an early stage of the computer network. A number of music programs involving analysis and sound generation are written in FORTRAN or one of its successors, FORTRAN II or FORTRAN IV.

Fortspinnung: A German term meaning melodic unfolding or spinning-out. Fortspinnung denotes a situation of more-or-less continuous development and transformation rather than repetition and is achieved by avoiding cadential junctures and clearly delineated phrase endings.

four-channel sound: See quadraphonic* sound.

Fourier analysis: The determination of the amplitude* and frequency* of each of the component sine* waves in a complex waveform*. This can be achieved either mathematically or by using an electronic device.

fourth chord: See quartal* chord.

fourth order set: A term originated by composer and theorist Milton Babbitt to designate a source* set that creates combinatorial* relationships at six different levels of transposition*. See combinatoriality*.

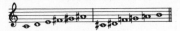

four-track recording: See multiple-track recording.

four-track tape recorder: A multiple-channel* tape* recorder that records four channels in the same direction as opposed to a quarter-track* (stereo*) tape recorder in which two are recorded in one direction and two in the other. A four-track tape recorder can record or play back four separate channels of audio* material at the same time. Tracks* are aligned as follows:

fractional meter: 1. A meter such as 4½/8 which equals 4/8 + 1/16 (see example a). Fractional meters are usually employed when the rhythmic pattern begins or ends with a half-beat. 2. A meter such as ⅔/4 equalizing two eighth notes of a triplet figure (see example b) minus the third note. The types of fractional meter listed above may be found in the works of such composers as Pierre Boulez (*Le Marteau sans Maître* [1955]), Edgar Varèse (*Integrales* [1925] and *Octandre* [1924]), and Wallingford Riegger (*Study in Sonority* [1927]).

a) $\frac{4½}{8}$ ♫♫♫   b) $\frac{⅔}{4}$ ♫ [♩]

fragmentation: The breaking-up of a musical motive or theme into smaller component units.

frame notation: A system of notation for chance* music that allows the performer to choose certain modes of operation within an established and regulated framework.

free atonality: Music written without a tonal center. This harmonic state was considered by composer Arnold Schoenberg to be a transitional phase between tonality and a more rigorously ordered system of twelve-tone* composition.

free resonance: The natural phenomenon that causes the vibrations of one body to set off vibrations in a second body when the two bodies respond to identical frequencies*. Free resonance differs from forced resonance in that the latter occurs when the primary vibration is transmitted by contact (e.g., from the vibrating string of a violin to its soundboard). Free resonance is easily demonstrated when one tuning fork is struck, setting off sympathetic vibrations in another tuning fork nearby.

frequency: The number of vibrations per unit of time of a sound source. Usually frequency is expressed in cycles per second or hertz*.

frequency band: A continuous range of frequencies* found between specified upper and lower limits.

frequency counter: A signal* frequency* measuring device that operates by counting the number of oscillations that occur within a designated period of time.

frequency generator: See oscillator*.

frequency modulation: 1. General: the recurring variation of the frequency* of a signal*. 2. Radio frequency: varying the frequency of a carrier wave in order to transmit a signal. 3. Audio frequency: periodic pitch variation.

frequency shift: A change in frequency* accomplished without altering the other characteristics (amplitude*, harmonics*, etc.) of a waveform*.

frequency shifter: An electronic device that changes the frequency* of a waveform* without altering its other characteristics (amplitude*, harmonics*, etc.).

French National Radio: The first organized experimental work in musique* concrète took place in the studios of French National Radio in Paris. Pierre Schaeffer began manipulating recorded sounds there soon after the Second World War. Some of the resulting works were broadcast in 1948 as a "concert of noise". In 1951 a special studio was created for Schaeffer and his colleagues Pierre Henry and Jacques Poullin. Other composers who later worked in the studio were Pierre Boulez and Karlheinz Stockhausen.

full-track tape recorder: A tape* recorder in which one tape* head spans the entire width of a quarter-inch magnetic* tape.

fundamental: The lowest pitch in a complex* tone.

futurism: An art movement started by poet and dramatist Francesco Marinetti in Italy before the First World War. Important futurist documents were written by Balilla Pratella in 1910 (*Manifesto of Futurist Musicians*) and in 1911 (*Technical Manifesto of Futurist Music*), and by Luigi Russolo in 1913 (*Futurist Manifesto*). Futurism as a credo heralded the significance of an art geared to the machine age (arte dei rumori). The futurists proclaimed a complete disassociation from all previous music and designed special noise instruments (amplified by megaphones) to reflect the new reality of sound in the twentieth century. *Pacific 231* (1924) by Arthur Honegger, with its sound of the railroad, may be interpreted as a musical work influenced by futurism. Musique* concrète and the general increase in the use of noise elements in all kinds of twentieth cen-

tury music may also be seen as reflecting the impact of this movement. See bruitism*, mechanistic* aesthetic.

fuzz bass: A sound common to rock* groups produced by an amplified electric bass* guitar channeled through a distortion booster. This sound is usually loud and sustained.

G

gain: The amount of amplification achieved in an electronic circuit*.

gamelan orchestra: A general term for the native performing ensembles found in Indonesia and Southeast Asia. A typical gamelan orchestra contains a great variety of percussion instruments along with stringed instruments and flutes. The music produced by these ensembles is typically heterophonic* and rhythmically quite complex. Many Western composers (e.g., Claude Debussy in *Pagodes* [1903] and Pierre Boulez in *Le Marteau sans Maître* [1955]) have been influenced by the gentle but enveloping sound of gamelan orchestras and have attempted to re-create their sound. See exoticism*.

game theory: A mathematical process based on probability* and strategy that is used to analyze problems and select courses of action when confronted with an opponent who is doing likewise. Game theory is used in computer* programming* as well as in various styles of avant-garde* composition.

gapped scale: A scale pattern taken out of the context of a larger scale structure.

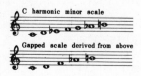

In Western music the pentatonic* scale may be viewed as a gapped scale of the larger diatonic pattern. Most of the scales employed in music of the Near and Far East are derivatives of a larger scale system.

gate: An electronic circuit* in which a signal* (or a set of electrical conditions) is used to control the passage of other signals. Gates are a part of most electronic systems including synthesizers* and computers*.

gating: The use of a signal (or a set of electrical conditions) to control the passage of other signals through a circuit*. Gating is a form of electronic switching common in synthesizers* and computers*.

Gaussian noise: See white* noise.

Gebrauchsmusik: Literally "music for use", indicating music of a practical and utilitarian nature that might be performed at home or in school as opposed to music of a more specialized and esoteric nature that would be found in a concert hall. The term first came into use in the 1920's in Germany, and is frequently associated with the composer Paul Hindemith. Gebrauchsmusik is generally more direct and less technically involved than concert music but has often been presented in the concert hall with good effect.

Gemeinschaftsmusik: A German term common in the 1930's that referred to music that was intended more-to be sung and played than to be listened to by an audience. Works of this type were often in a polyphonic style with each voice given equal importance, so that all performers could participate fully in the "community" musical experience. Paul Hindemith's *Das Neue Werk* (1927) consisted of compositions of this kind. See Gebrauchsmusik*.

generation: A stage in a multiple recording process. The first recording is spoken of as a first generation recording, the second recording (or re-recording) is spoken of as a second generation recording, etc. See tape* recorder.

generator: An electronic instrument that is capable of originating a signal*. See oscillator*, random* generator.

geometric abstractionism: An art movement related to cubism* that originated in the early twentieth century and was concerned with simple geometric shapes such as circles, rectangles, arcs, and straight lines. Geometric abstractionism is sometimes referred to as classical abstractionism because of its stylistic similarity to the Geometric Period of Hellenic Art (900-700 B.C.). Pioneering artists in this style were Kasimir Malevich and Piet Mondrian. The neo-classical* movement in music in which Igor Stravinsky and others were involved was an outgrowth of the same artistic viewpoint—a return to the classical ideals of symmetry, proportion, and balance.

Gerausch: A German acoustical term denoting very dissonant noise.

Geschlossenheit: A German term indicating the unity and logic found in the form of a musical work.

Gestalt: In music this term refers to the form or shape of a work (or one of its parts) perceived as a unified entity rather than as a collection of elements.

ghost note: A note that is fingered but barely blown in jazz*, creating an almost inaudible sound. Usually ghost notes are found in long and rapid melodic passages played by trumpeters or reed instrument players.

glasses: Any glass object that produces sound. Usually sounds on glasses are produced either by striking the glass with a beater or rubbing it with damp fingers. The use of water glasses filled to different levels is found as early as 1746 in a work such as Gluck's *Concerto Upon Twenty-six Drinking Glasses*. Tuned glass bowls were common in the eighteenth century and many composers of the twentieth century have used glass devices with great effect. Henry Cowell in his *Concerto for Percussion and Orchestra* (1958-9) included five porcelain bowls; Haubenstock-Ramati scored four crystal tumblers in his *Symphonies de Timbres* (1957); and Bo Nilsson used empty glass bottles in his *Reaktionen* for four percussionists (1960). Harry Partch has experimented extensively with glass instruments, as in his invention of cloud* chamber bowls.

gospel jazz: Jazz* based on gospel songs. The gospel song often falls into a call-and-response pattern, and is an exuberant type of music characterized by hand-clapping and foot-stomping.

graph notation: A system of notation used in aleatoric* and electronic* music in which instructions are given on graph paper. The individual squares or boxes* on the paper sometimes have time significance. See frame* notation and directive* graphics.

graphic notation: Visual symbols used in place of traditional notes and rests to indicate musical ideas in aleatoric*, multimedia*, and electronic* scores. Graphic notation usually generalizes phrase shape, dynamics, pitch contour, and rhythmic patterns into geometric designs. While most composers have recognized the need for new notational systems, a great problem lies in the fact that, at the present time, there seems to be little coordina-

tion of new developments in notation. Hence, the performer of new music is often faced with the tedious job of studying an entirely new technique of notation before a note can be played. See frame* notation, directive* graphics, klavarscribo*.

Grossmutterakkord: A term used by Nicolas Slonimsky to denote a chord containing all twelve notes of the chromatic scale and eleven different intervals. The interval that divides the structure at its midpoint is the tritone and the intervals formed from the midpoint moving toward both ends are inversions of each other.

growl: An effect common in jazz* and some avant-garde* music in which a rasping sound is produced on a given tone. The effect is common on brass instruments and is produced by making an actual growling sound at the back of the throat while playing a note. The growl is often employed while the player uses a plunger mute and is usually indicated by the following notation:

Grundbrechung: A term from Schenkerian* analysis that indicates the horizontal projection of a fundamental triad in the bass voice. The

Grundbrechung and Urlinie* together constitute the Ursatz*, or "fundamental setting". See Schenkerian* analysis.

Grundgestalt: 1. The phrase, theme or germ idea that is the basis of a musical composition. 2. The basic set* or series* in twelve-tone* technique complete with rhythm, accent, etc. Composer Arnold Schoenberg is credited with first using the term in this way.

Grundreihe: German for the basic form of a twelve-tone* row (set*, series*) before it undergoes transformation* or transposition*. Also referred to as the prime* or original* form of the row.

gushing chords: Short and full glissando runs on the harp, indicated by the notation below:

gutbucket: A manner or style of playing jazz* often described as "dirty", earthy and/or "down home". For a brass player the use of mutes and plungers, especially when coupled with growls* and various other distortions of tone, help to effect the gutbucket style. A gutbucket was a bucket that caught drippings (called gutterings) from gin barrels.

H

H⁻: Symbol for Hauptstimme.*

hai-ku: A very short Japanese poem employing great expressiveness in a few words. The concept of brevity and unity found in such poems has attracted twentieth century composers who have created musical works in the same spirit of economy, or who have set the words of the hai-ku to music.

half-track tape recorder: See two-track* tape recorder.

half-valve: A technique common to jazz* in which a brass player (e.g., trumpet or valve trombone) depresses a valve halfway, producing a tone of uncertain pitch and definition.

Hammond organ: An electronic musical instrument similar in size and conformation to a spinet piano that was first marketed by the Hammond Instrument Company in 1935. A keyboard controls small rotary generators* that produce electrical oscillations corresponding in frequency* to the pitches of the tempered scale. Harmonic* controls make a large number of timbres possible. This instrument is frequently used in churches, funeral parlors, and popular music performances.

hamograph: An electronic control device developed at the University of Toronto Electronic Studio for use in the creation of electronic* music. The hamograph is a rhythm-amplitude control instrument that is used in liaison with tape* recorders, sound generators, and band-pass* filters to realize different parameters* of a pre-planned score simultaneously. The device coordinates pitch, rhythm, timbre*, and spatial effects with the help of independent multiple loudspeaker* units in as many as six separate voices.

happening: A musical, theatrical, or multimedia* event* which is carried out partially or wholly in random fashion. There may or may not be a guiding, overall idea in evidence. Many happenings are random collections of small structured or unstructured elements such as readings, musical pieces, photographic projections, records, dance, and paintings. See aleatory*.

hard bop: An offshoot of the bop* movement that attempted to regain the emotional fervor of the earliest bop music via the use of gospel tunes and traditional blues* as the basis for improvisation*. This movement came in reaction to the transformation of bop in the West Coast (California) school during the 1950's as played by musicians such as Shorty Rogers, Chet Baker, Dave Brubeck and Jimmy Giuffre. East Coast musicians such as Art Blakey, Horace Silver, Billy Taylor and Thelonius Monk led the hard bop movement (sometimes described as "funky" style). See East* Coast jazz, progressive* jazz.

hard copy: Data printed by a computer* that is in a more or less permanent and humanly readable form.

hard rock: A term often applied to the early rock* music of performers such as Bill Haley and the Comets, Elvis Presley, Little Richard, and Chubby Checker during the 1950's. Hard rock is characterized by a driving, monotonous beat, basic chord progressions using I, IV, and V, repetitive musical phrases; and lyrics that often border on the inane. In the late 1960's, performers James Brown and Janis Joplin managed to capture the vitality of hard rock and at the same time incorporate more musical sophistication into the overall form.

hardware: The electronic, magnetic, mechanical, and electrical components that comprise a computer*.

harmonic: A partial* whose frequency* is related to the fundamental* by integer multiples such as 1, 2, 3, etc. For example, if a fundamental vibrates at 100 Hz* the next harmonic will vibrate at 200 Hz and the third harmonic at 300 Hz. See harmonic* series.

harmonic analyzer: An electronic device used to calculate the relative strength of all the partials* present in a complex waveform*.

harmonic canon I: A string instrument built by composer Harry Partch in 1945 at the University of Wisconsin. The instrument is thirty-seven inches high at the back and twenty-eight inches high at the front, creating a sloped panel on which two sets of forty-four guitar strings are strung on two different levels. The two planes of strings intersect and may be used either separately or together.

harmonic canon II: A string instrument similar to harmonic* canon I built by composer Harry Partch in 1953. The instrument is primarily wood (Sitka spruce, oak, spruce, and redwood) and has large resonating chambers. It is thirty-six inches high at the back and thirty inches high at the front. Guitar and mandolin strings are used in two planes of forty-four strings.

harmonic cluster: A tone-cluster* formed by silently depressing a given number of piano keys and thus creating sympathetic vibrations.

harmonic crescendo: An increase in harmonic tension described by composer Paul Hindemith with regard to harmonic* fluctuation.

harmonic diminuendo: A decrease in harmonic tension described by composer Paul Hindemith with regard to harmonic* fluctuation.

harmonic distortion: The intended or unintended introduction of additional overtones* during the electronic processing of a signal*.

harmonic dualism: An acoustic-aesthetic theory which holds that music will always contain the concepts of consonance and dissonance to represent basic polarities found in the laws of nature and human experience, even though they may assume relative positions with regard to one another in a constant process of change. This is a view held by theorist Joseph Yasser, and it should not be confused with the dualistic theory of the equality of major and minor as set forth by Jean Philippe Rameau, Hugo Riemann, Moritz Hauptman, and others.

harmonic echo: An echo effect in which one or more upper partials* are sounded without the presence of the fundamental*.

harmonic fluctuation: Composer Paul Hindemith's term from the *Craft of Musical Composition* (1941) for a classification of chords in relation to how they interact with one another in harmonic flow. Chords are grouped in six basic categories. A movement from a chord belonging to a higher or more "valuable" group (e.g., a chord without seconds or sevenths) to a chord of a lower group (e.g., a chord containing a tritone) represents an increase in tension. A movement in the opposite direction would constitute a decrease in tension. This up-and-down movement of tension and change of stability results in harmonic fluctuation, which Hindemith also refers to as a type of harmonic* crescendo or diminuendo. See series* I.

harmonic litany: A term used by French composer Oliver Messiaen to refer to the repetition of a line or a fragment of a line with different harmonization.

harmonic monism: Theorist Joseph Yasser's premise that the division of intervals into consonances and dissonances is essentially meaningless because of the relative stance these concepts take when juxtaposed in a particular style or idiom.

harmonic planes: A general term referring to harmonic materials separated in a composition by key (as in a bitonal* or bichordal* texture), register, rhythmic content, orchestration, or timbral difference. A work such as *Three-Score Set* (1943) by William Schuman illustrates the concept of harmonic planes particularly well.

harmonic series: A composite of the many harmonics* that vibrate along with the fundamental* in a complex* tone. It should be noted that only harmonics 2, 4, and 8 conform with equal temperament.

harmonic synthesis: The technique of combining divergent chordal structures (both tonal and atonal*) into a viable, unified harmonic scheme.

Hauptrhythmus: A German term indicating an outstanding or especially significant rhythmic pattern in a musical work. The term is used primarily in connection with twelve-tone* music, and is indicated by the letters HR marked in the score.

Hauptstimme: A German term meaning principal voice. Arnold Schoenberg used Hauptstimme (and its abbreviation H⁻) to indicate a particular line that should predominate in a contrapuntal texture.

Hausmusik: A German term meaning music to be played at home. Generally Hausmusik is not technically demanding and was typically written for instruments with piano accompaniment, recorder, or violin. See Gebrauchsmusik*.

head arrangement: A jazz* arrangement worked out with a minimum of notes written for the performers. Instead, the piece is thought out between the players through consultation and an exchange of musical ideas. The "memorized" version is then performed.

headphones: Electronic sound receivers that can be worn on the head. Headphones can be attached to one or both ears.

head-riff: A main theme or motive in jazz* that is played by the melodic instruments at the beginning of the piece, often in unison. Improvisation* based on the harmonic and melodic structure of the theme follows, until a point is reached where the theme is reiterated once more, bringing the work to a conclusion. The head-riff is often based on a set of blues* changes*.

hellertion: An electronic* musical instrument developed by Bruno Hellberger and Peter Lertes in 1928 which is operated by ribbon* controllers similar to the trautonium*.

hemitonic music: Any music based on a scale comprised of half-steps.

heptad: A vertical* sonority consisting of seven different pitches.

heptatonic scale: Any scale consisting of seven different tones within an octave. Traditional diatonic scales (major and minor scales, the church modes, etc.) fall within this category.

hertz: A term that has been adopted internationally as a substitute for cycles* per second (the number of complete vibrations per unit of time). The name is derived from the nineteenth century German scientist Heinrich Hertz, who first recognized, created, and measured electro-magnetic waves. One hertz is equal to one cycle per second.

heterodyne: The process whereby two signals* of different frequencies* are combined in order to produce two other frequencies equal to the sum and difference of the original frequencies. For example, a 400 Hz* signal combined with a 100 Hz signal would produce frequencies of 500 Hz (sum) and 300 Hz (difference).

heterometric: Extreme freedom and independence of meter and rhythm in the component voices or parts of a composition. See polymeter*.

heteronomous music: A term coined by Iannis Xenakis to denote the concept of external conflict that is present when two opposing orchestras or instrumentalists are set against each other and influence the response of one another in a competitive or contradictory fashion. Xenakis claims that this type of game or duel may be summarized by a matrix conforming to the mathematical game* theory. An example of such music would be improvisational tabla or sitar playing in Indian music whereby each player attempts to confuse or outdo the others within a specific framework of musical style.

heterophony: 1. Slight variations in a single melodic line as performed by two or more players operating simultaneously. 2. A kind of "superpolyphony" in which the relative harmonic and melodic independence of the parts is stressed. Some aleatory* or serial* music may exhibit this kind of freedom of the component parts.

hexachord: 1. A term stemming from Medieval music theory that indicates a specific modal pattern of six tones. 2. Hexachord in the modern sense has come to indicate the six pitches that are stated in the first half (or the second) of a given twelve-tone* row.

hexad: A vertical* sonority consisting of six different pitches.

hexagram: A symbol consisting of six whole or divided lines used in the *I Ching**, an ancient Chinese book of divination.

Composers of chance* music have used the hexagrams of the *I Ching* to arrive at or manipulate musical material.

hexatonic scale: A scale consisting of six different tones within an octave. One possible hexatonic scale is shown in the example below. The whole-tone* scale is also a hexatonic scale.

hi-fi: See high* fidelity.

high fidelity: Sound reproduction of high quality that strives to reproduce the "live" musical sound with as much accuracy as possible. Stereo* sound and quadraphonic* sound are some of the more recent innovations in the field of high fidelity.

high-pass filter: An electronic filter* that allows frequencies* above a given cutoff point to pass through while attenuating* severely all frequencies below that point.

hi-hat: Also known as a foot or "sock" cymbal, the hi-hat is a pair of cymbals, usually thirteen to fifteen inches in diameter operated by a foot pedal. The drummer often uses the hi-hat to emphasize the weak beats of the measure in jazz*.

Hintergrund: German for background* as used in Schenkerian* analysis.

hinweisende notation: See directive* graphics.

hirajoshi scale: A pentatonic* scale of Eastern derivation.

hiss: See tape* hiss.

Höherlegung: An octave transfer in Schenkerian* analysis.

honky-tonk: Honky-tonk is synonymous with barrelhouse*. The term refers to a style of ragtime* piano playing as performed in dance halls, gin mills, or houses of prostitution in New Orleans in the early decades of the century. Honky-tonk style was typically loud, gaudy, and somewhat tinny sounding due to the poor quality of the pianos found in these establishments.

horizontalism: A term coined by theorist Felix Salzer to denote a kind of Schenkerian* prolongation* in which the intervals of a given chord are filled in by contrapuntal motion in the outer melodic voices.

hot jazz: A vague and general jazz* term usually applied to one of the many varieties of dixieland*.

HR: Abbreviation for Hauptrhythmus*.

hum: A steady low-range sound sometimes found in the amplifier* of a high* fidelity system, produced by the alternating current power-frequency* and its harmonics*.

Hungarian scale: A seven-tone scale stemming from Hungarian folk music that is found in two forms: Hungarian major (example a below) and Hungarian minor (example b below):

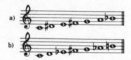

hyperchromaticism: A term sometimes used to describe music based on microtones*.

Hz: Abbreviation for hertz*.

I

I: Abbreviation for inversion*.

I Ching: The *I Ching* — or, as it is commonly known in English, the *Book of Changes* — is a Chinese manual of divination written some time before 1000 B.C. Included in the book are interpretations of 64 hexagrams* which are formed by the manipulation of stalks. Chance composers such as John Cage have used the

I Ching to arrive at and work with musical materials in a random fashion. See chance* music, aleatory*.

ILLIAC computer: A computer* used at the University of Illinois in the mid-1950's by L. A. Hiller, Jr. and L. M. Issacson for experiments in musical composition. See MUSI-COMP*.

imbroglio: A term sometimes used to describe polymetric* or polyrhythmic* textures. In a more traditional context the term is usually applied to operatic scenes in which the singers are operating in essentially contrasting meters or rhythms, creating a feeling of confusion and entanglement.

IML: An acronym for Intermediary Musical Language, a computer* programming* language developed by Hubert Howe, Alexander Jones, and Michael Kassler at Princeton University. IML uses only the forty-eight characters of the standard keypunch* machine to encode musical information for processing by computer.

impedence: The amount of resistance to the flow of alternating current* present in an electronic circuit*.

imperfections technique: A random method of arriving at material for a musical composition by tracing the points of imperfection found on a piece of translucent paper directly onto manuscript paper where they are formed into notes. John Cage used this technique in *Music for Piano* (1952). See aleatory*, chance* operations.

implicit musical graphics: Graphic* notation that is not specific in intent. See frame* notation and directive* graphics.

impressionism: A movement in art, literature, and music of the late nineteenth century. The paintings of Claude Monet, Edward Manet, and Pierre Auguste Renoir attempted to capture the very spirit of light on the canvas, and to depict the "impression", but not necessarily with great attention to realistic detail. In a similar fashion, poets such as Pierre Charles Baudelaire, Stéphane Mallarmé, and Arthur Rimbaud strove for the direct experience conveyed by words. In music Claude Debussy is generally conceded to be the foremost impressionistic composer, and his interest in exotic scale forms, whole-tone* scales, pentatonic* scales, and modes coupled with chord parallelism* and extension (chords of the seventh, ninth*, and thirteenth*) created an effect in music of lush understatement, ambiguity, and freedom. Impressionistic composers generally favored brief thematic melodies, the use of plagal cadences, root movement avoiding fourths and fifths, unusual instrumental combinations, and a miniaturization of form. The tone poem and prelude virtually replaced the multi-movement symphony and the sonata. Other composers often identified as impressionists include Frederick Delius, Charles Loeffler, Charles Griffes, Edward MacDowell, and Maurice Ravel, although each of these men had his own distinct and different approach to music, which makes a categorization of all of them as "impressionists" a sizeable over-generalization if further clarification is not specified.

improvisation: The spontaneous creation of new or modified musical expression by a performer or a group of performers. Many twentieth century composers have written sections of works and even whole works in which improvisation is specified. Also, groups of performers under the leadership of such composer-performers as Lukas Foss have banded together to produce entire programs of improvised pieces. Depending on the circumstances and the wishes of the composer (if there is one), performers may or may not be furnished with musical material, or an outline or framework of some kind, as a point of departure. Improvisation is the heart of jazz* and was common in this idiom before its rebirth in twentieth century concert music.

impulse: A sudden, brief surge of voltage* or current* having no definite pitch or timbre*. One use of an impulse is as a trigger* for some activity within a computer* or synthesizer*.

inaudible music: Music written for electronic instruments that consists of pitches that are above or below the audio* spectrum. Multimedia* works that are visual and soundless also fall into this category. Early twentieth century composers such as Nicolas Obukhov and Michael Magne were among the first to experiment with inaudible music. Obukhov designed "crystal" and "ether" instruments for this purpose, (they were never built) and Magne composed his Symphonie Humaine with both an audible and inaudible version. John Cage's 4'33" (1952), a work for any combination of instruments, is to be performed silently in three movements. These, and other works of the avant-garde*, such as La Monte Young's Composition 1960 #6 in which the performers sit and stare at each other and the audience, may be categorized as inaudible music.

indeterminacy: A term often employed in connection with aleatoric* music, in which a composer may splatter ink on a page of manuscript paper and play the "notes" thereupon produced, or use some other arbitrary method (dice, dominoes, etc.) in order to achieve a plan for a musical composition. John Cage has stated that indeterminacy implies a new concept of art, one removed from conventional boundaries and conceived through new means largely outside the intellectual control of the composer. See chance* music, aleatory*.

indicative notation: A style of notation in which the composer indicates approximate pitches, durations, activities, etc. giving the performer some freedom in interpretation. See graphic* notation.

infinite baffle: A loudspeaker* system with no air path between the front and the back of the speaker cone.

information theory: A theory concerned with the statistical analysis of the efficiency of communications systems. It is based on the science of probability* and deals with flow, channels, disturbances, and other factors affecting information transmission. At first, information theory was used primarily to study telecommunication and computers* but now it is applied to all kinds of information networks.

infra: A prefix relating the word that follows to the infra-diatonic* scale described by theorist Joseph Yasser.

infra-diatonic scale: Theorist Joseph Yasser's term for a scale containing five regular (C, D, F, G, A) and two auxiliary degrees (E and B) giving it a 5+2 "formula". The regular degrees correspond to a pentatonic* scale and the latter two are close in pitch to E and B of the diatonic scale. Yasser calls this scale one of the "lower order", meaning that it represents a fundamental stage in scalar designs. He states that in many cultures employing the basic pentatonic scale one often finds the auxiliary pitches E and B, just as the five chromatic tones serve as auxiliary degrees to our diatonic scale. The auxiliary degrees in the infra-diatonic scale are used for purposes of melodic embellishment, and they may be omitted without any detriment to a given melodic structure.

inharmonic partial: An upper partial*
not in the harmonic* series of the
fundamental*. The closer the in-
harmonics lie to the fundamental
the more noise-like are their quality.
The more inharmonic partials that
are mixed into a sound of definite
pitch, the more distorted that pitch
will become.

input: 1. Electrical energy or information in other forms that is applied
to an electronic circuit* or device.
2. The mechanical connection through
which information is fed into an
electronic system.

Inselbildung: A name given by composer Arnold Schoenberg to passages in which formal elements are
replaced by the free association of
musical ideas.

intensity curve: See envelope*.

interchangeability: 1. Musical lines,
sections, or movements that can be
performed in various sequences resulting in a constantly variable work
of art. In Pierre Boulez's *Third
Piano Sonata* (1957) there are five
sections that can be played in any
order as long as the longest section is
in the middle. 2. The phenomenon
that exists when a twelve-tone* row
is written so that its first hexachord*
can be combined with a hexachord
of one of the row's transformations*
or transpositions*. See combinatoriality*.

intercut: An editing process used in
film* music for adjusting timing and
removing mistakes. The tracks* must
be precisely cut and spliced so that
they will remain in synchronization.

interface: An element of a synthesizer*
or computer* that allows sections of
the electronic system with dissimilar
characteristics to operate in conjunction.

inter-media: See multimedia* art.

International Composer's Guild: A New
York City-based group of composers
of various nationalities that pre-

sented programs of experimental music during the 1920's under the
direction of Edgar Varèse. The
Guild, which was the first modern
music society organized in the
United States, was in close contact
with similar groups in Europe.

internationalism: A term applied to a
style of experimental music of the
1920's that emanated from composers associated with the International* Composer's Guild.

**International Society for Contempo-
rary Music:** An organization formed
in Salzburg in 1922 for the purpose
of presenting new music of all na-
tions at annual festivals. Prominent
musicians from various countries
were invited to perform and submit
works. Most ISCM festivals were
held in Europe, but in 1941 and
1942 they were held in the United
States because of the war.

interruption: Theorist Felix Salzer uses
this term to denote a special architectonic* device that divides a structural unit. For example, a point of
interruption may be achieved by
the use of a dominant chord in a
tonal progression that is supported
by inconclusive melodic elements
that do not lead immediately to a
definitive, closing cadence. Interruption divides a structural unit into
distinct, subsidiary parts or units,
usually of an antecedent-consequent
nature. Theorist Allen Forte uses the
term in a very similar way, meaning deflection from a goal.

intersection: A phenomenon that occurs when any two musical structures share a common element. For
example, a Db major scale and an
F major scale would have three
points of intersection: on the pitches
F, Bb, and C which are present in
both scales.

intertonal gravitation: A term coined
by theorist Joseph Yasser that is
basically synonymous with tonality.

interval ambit: 1. The amount of frequency* difference between two pitches. 2. The number of different linear intervals used in a musical passage or work.

interval class: A term coined by Milton Babbitt that denotes those intervals regarded as equivalent in twelve-tone* technique. All of the intervals below would belong to the same interval class.

Major 3rd   Major 10th   Major 3rd   Minor 6th   Minor 13th
                        (by inversion) (inversion
                                        of previous
                                        Major 3rd)

intervallic cell: See basic* cell.

interval variation: The altering of a musical motive or theme accomplished by revising the interval structure. In the following example from Béla Bartók's *Sixth String Quartet* (1939), a motive first stated in the first violin is later varied in the viola:

interval-vector: A numerical representation of the intervallic content of a given set*. The set F♯, A, B♭, and B would be represented by the pitch* numbers 0, 3, 4, 5. The numbers refer to the number of semitones that A, B♭ and B are found to be located above F♯ (0). This set contains the following interval classes: two minor seconds, one major second, one minor third, one major third (enharmonic diminished fourth), one perfect fourth, and no perfect fifths. Thus, the interval vector of this set would then be expressed by the following integers: 2 1 1 1 1 0.

invariant: An element that is constant and remains unaffected by the operations under consideration. In twelve-tone* technique invariants

are the properties of a tone* row that remain the same when the row is transformed through inversion*, retrograde*, or transposition*. Probably the most common instance of invariance occurs when a row is transposed. Pitches change but the sequence of the interval structure remains the same.

intonarumori: Early acoustical noise instruments that produced growls, howls, roars, gurgles, etc. Intonarumori were hand-activated and the sound was projected by means of horns and megaphones. These instruments were used in 1914 on one of Luigi Russolo's "art of noise" concerts. See futurism*.

inversion: 1. the altering of a motive, line, or twelve-tone* row by changing each ascending interval to a descending interval and vice versa, (see example a below). 2. The placing of one tone or line above or below another tone or line (see example b below). See mirror*, involution*, reflective* chord.

invertibility: The structural design of a hexachord* of a twelve-tone* row that makes it possible to create through exact inversion* a second hexachord which at some interval of transposition* will duplicate no notes of the original hexachord. See combinatoriality*.

involution: Composer Howard Hanson's term for mirror* inversion, which may take three forms: 1. Simple: the involuted chord differs in sound from the given chord. For example, a D major triad when inverted by exact interval forms a G minor triad (example a); 2. Isometric: the involuted chord has the same kind of sound as the original sonority. For example, the tetrad* C E G B when inverted forms a major seventh chord also, with the notes Db, F, Ab, C (example b); 3. Enharmonic: the involuted sonority and the original contain the same notes in different octaves, with the exception of one common tone. For example, the augmented triad D, F♯, A♯ involutes to produce another augmented chord (Gb, Bb, D) that contains two enharmonic equivalents with the original chord (Gb/F♯ and Bb/A♯) (example c). See reflective* chord.

IO: An abbreviation that denotes an inverted twelve-tone* row which begins on the first note of the original* row.

irrational rhythm: See time* fields.

ISCM: See International* Society for Contemporary Music.

isomelody: See isomelos*.

isomelos: The repetition of a melodic pattern with varying rhythm.

isomeric sonority: Composer Howard Hanson's term for sonorities containing the same intervals that are not involutions* of one another. The chords found below both contain one perfect fifth, one major third, one minor third, one major second, one minor second, and one tritone, but they are not mirrors* of one another.

isometric sonority: Composer Howard Hanson's term for sonorities formed by the combination of a chord with its involution*, resulting in the same intervallic structure when read from bottom to top or top to bottom. The

chord found below illustrates this principle.

isorhythm: The repetition of a rhythmic pattern, usually over a fairly long period of time. The term has an extensive historical background, and is usually found in connection with music of the fourteenth and fifteenth centuries. Many contemporary composers have turned to the device as a way of achieving unity without relying on a more familiar type of rhythmic design. Isorhythm has been particularly helpful as a means of organization for many twelve-tone* composers.

isotrophy: A term coined by Iannis Xenakis to denote regions or groups of sounds that balance each other by moving in both ascending and descending directions simultaneously without any one sound or group of sounds having a "privileged" direction to take. A static type of sound emerges from such a situation.

IT: An abbreviation used to indicate a transposed inversion* of a twelve-tone* row.

J

jack: A socket (female) used to receive a plug (male) for connecting or continuing an electronic circuit*. See patch* panel, patch* cord.

jam: Group improvisation* by jazz* musicians, as in a "jam session". This improvisation may be soloistic at times, with each player taking his appointed turn, or it may be improvisation by the group as a whole on familiar jazz tunes, or very commonly, on the blues*. Jam sessions connote informality and occur generally in a social rather than a professional context.

jazz: A generic term used to cover all

the various kinds of music such as dixieland*, swing*, bop*, progressive* jazz, ragtime*, bossa* nova, etc. The precise origin of the word is unclear. It first appears around 1914, and may be derived from the Creole word jass, a term used in connection with the conga dances performed in New Orleans at that time. Although it is difficult to generalize musically with regard to all of the varieties of jazz, the following can be stated as basic traits of jazz music: 1. a steady, regular pulse background (often in 4/4) is usually present, over which the eighth note (not the quarter note) becomes the basic rhythmic unit; 2. a forward-propelling rhythmic directionality is found, usually creating a strong emphasis on the weak beats (back-beats) such as two and four in a quadruple meter. The sense of directionality is often referred to as the "swing" of jazz; 3. a tendency to attack almost all of the notes is common in jazz, as opposed to other kinds of music in which a true legato technique is more appropriate; 4. the rhythm of jazz is almost impossible to notate in conventional terms. In the example below the rhythm indicated at (a) would be played as falling somewhere between the two rhythms indicated at (b); 5. improvisation* is the wellspring of jazz; 6. syncopation is more important in jazz than rhythmic regularity; 7. a sense of humor often pervades jazz music. See appendix under Jazz and Popular Music for a listing of jazz terms in this volume.

Jeune France: A group of French composers consisting of Yves Baudrier, André Jolivet, Oliver Messiaen, and Daniel Lesur who united in 1936 to devote themselves to a new music free from academic and revolutionary formulas. Jeune France hoped to encourage the development of young French composers by giving their works a chance to be heard. The group also wanted to encourage performances of French scores that had been ignored in the past. Messiaen and Lesur were the leading figures of the group, although Jolivet was important in bringing to the attention of the other three composers his interest in non-Western music.

jitterbugging: A dancing style common to the 1940's and 1950's in which strenuous physical motions on the parts of the participants were common. Often the female was thrown or lifted into the air by her partner. Swing* music usually provided the background for jitterbugging sessions.

joystick: A controller* that allows two or more potential voltage* sources to be manipulated independently, simultaneously, or in direct relationship to each other, by means of a vertical lever that can be rotated a full 360 degrees.

K

kaleidophon: An early electronic* musical instrument built by Jörg Mager in Germany that was a descendent of the sphärophon* and the partiturophon*. The kaleidophon was used extensively in theatrical productions of its day until being destroyed in World War II.

Kansas City style: Jazz* music indigenous to the Kansas City area during the late 1920's and 1930's. Kansas City style became important after the jazz movements in New* Orleans and Chicago*. Since Kansas City lacked enterprises such as recording companies and publishing houses the musicians there were able to produce a music free of some of the negative influences of commercialism. Kansas City style placed a greater emphasis on melodic development, a lighter overall sound, and improvisational experiments. It had a strong influence on later developments such as bop* and big-band* swing*. Some musicians important to Kansas City style include Lester Young, Charlie Parker, George and Julia Lee, Charlie Christian, Herschel Evans, Bennie Moten, and Jim Daddy Walker.

Keimzelle theory: A theory developed by the Dutch composer Willem Pijper in which an entire composition is derived from a small but potent harmonic and melodic cell. Pijper was a major composer in Holland, and his works include symphonies and many piano pieces. He also was the editor of *De Muziek*, an outstanding music journal, and the teacher of many notable composers such as Henk Badings, Rudolf Escher, and Hans Henkemans.

keyboard controller: An electronic device similar in appearance to a piano keyboard that generates specific control voltage* when a key is depressed. Keyboard controllers are a part of most electronic music synthesizers*.

key click: Sound produced when a player strikes a key on his instrument with force, resulting in a hard metallic click. This device is sometimes found in avant-garde* scores, and usually is indicated in the score by the sign +.

key punch: A device used to encode information on data* cards by creating perforation patterns that can be sensed and interpreted by a computer* or synthesizer*.

kHz: An abbreviation for kilohertz*.

kilohertz: A unit of frequency* equal to 1,000 cycles* per second or hertz*.

kinetic art: A term used to designate works such as mobiles (with or with-out motors), constructions set in motion by magnetic force, or assemblages of glass or metal that create patterns of light and shadow as they move. Important artists in this movement include Pol Bury, Julio Le Parc, George Richey, Yaacow Agam and Bryan Winter.

kithara I: An instrument invented by composer Harry Partch that stands about six feet tall. The instrument contains seven sound boards of redwood and uses seventy-two strings (guitar, tenor guitar and banjo), with pitch set by guitar tuning heads. As the strings are plucked the base resonates. The kithara I is the forerunner of the kithara* II, and was built between 1938 and 1943.

kithara II: An instrument that evolved from the kithara* I which stands over seven and a half feet high and may be played by one or more performers. The kithara II is broader at the base than at the top, and has large sounding boards made of Sitka spruce. It is built almost entirely out of wood, and it utilizes guitar, tenor guitar and banjo strings. Basically the instrument resembles the Greek kithara on a larger scale, as does the earlier instrument, the kithara* I.

kitsch: Art or music of slight aesthetic value, usually marked by the influence of popular taste, slickness, sentimentality, and sensationalism.

Klangfarbe: A German term meaning tone color or timbre*.

Klangfarbenmelodie: A German term used to indicate a linear compositional technique in which successive notes or chords are each assigned a different instrumental color. One of the first instances of Klangfarbenmelodie can be found in the third movement, "Farben", of Arnold Schoenberg's *Five Pieces for Orchestra*, Op. 16 (1909). Anton Webern used the technique in *Six Bagatelles for String Quartet*, Opus 9 (1913),

and Alban Berg in the last movement of *Lyric Suite* (1926) states
the opening phrase of the prelude to
Tristan in various string colors.
Elliott Carter, in *Etude No. 7 of
Eight Etudes and a Fantasy
for Woodwind Quartet* (1950) uses
Klangfarbenmelodie isolated from
pitch change. Only one pitch is employed (first line G), leaving the creation of musical expression solely to
the elements of timbre* and dynamics.

Klangfarben technique: See Klangfarbenmelodie*.

Klangumwandler: An electronic device
developed in the studios of South-
west German Radio in Baden-Baden
that is similar in operation to a ring*
modulator with one set of resultant
frequencies* suppressed.

Klavarscribo: A new notational system
devised by the Dutch musician
Cornelius Pot that replaces traditional durational notation with proportional graphic* notation. Pitch is
indicated by the use of horizontal
lines and accidentals are entirely
eliminated by using different note
heads for all twelve chromatic tones.
The system is read from top to bottom instead of from left to right as
in conventional notational systems.
Klavarscribo is an Esperanto word
meaning keyboard writing.

kua: The system of eight symbolic images that forms the foundation for
the *I Ching**.

Kulturbolschevismus: A term that
classifies all advanced and radical
art movements as having a Communist origin and impetus. Using this
credo as a rallying point, the Nazis
banned works by Arnold Schoenberg, Alban Berg, and Anton Webern
during their stay in power.

kumoi scale: A five-note (pentatonic)
scale stemming from Asian music
that has the following interval structure:

L

laser: A high-intensity beam of light
used to trigger oscillators* and other
electronic sound or visual equipment in multimedia* art. The beam
is aimed at a photoelectric receiving
unit connected to the equipment and
when a person or object breaks the
beam by passing through it the
equipment is turned either on or
off.

layering: The building of musical texture through the stratification of differing rhythmic patterns, methods of
pitch organization, and tone colors.
Contrasting rhythmic-melodic ideas
are combined one over the other to
produce a unified but internally
varying texture.

leader tape: White tape that is spliced
onto regular magnetic* tape to mark
the location of specific recorded passages and to serve as a lead-in at
the beginning of a reel.

lead sheet: The melody line, chord
symbols, and lyrics of a popular song
or jazz* tune printed on a sheet
typically used by a vocalist or pian-
ist in preparation for performance.

League of Composers: A New York
based society concerned with contemporary music that was formed in
1923 by a group of composers who
banded together to sponsor programs of new music. The League
was a splinter group of the International* Composers Guild. These
two organizations were the fore-
runners of the many contemporary
music groups of the 1960's and
1970's. Some composers who were
associated with the League in its
early years are Béla Bartók, Ernest
Bloch, Arthur Honegger, Darius Milhaud, Ottorino Respighi, and Egon
Wellesz.

leakage: Any random, unwanted sound that finds its way into a microphone*.

lick: A short phrase or riff* in jazz*.

light show: The use of theatrical lighting effects and abstract visual patterns on film or slides in a concert situation. Light shows often accompany dance, music, and theater performances in multimedia* presentations.

linear controller: An electronic device capable of continuously varying the characteristics of a sound. Linear controllers are used to generate an infinitely variable control voltage* as opposed to keyboard* controllers that generate discrete stepped control voltages. See ribbon* controller.

linear counterpoint: See dissonant* counterpoint.

liquidation: A term coined by Leopold Spinner to indicate the process of omitting motivic elements of an original phrase in later statements, reducing the original structure in size. Hence, liquidation is a developmental technique in which compression of musical ideas takes place.

Lissajous figure: The pattern produced on an oscilloscope* screen or television set when two different sine* waves are applied simultaneously to the horizontal and vertical deflection plates of the cathode-ray tube.

live-electronic music: Music in which certain aspects are created and modified by electronic equipment at the time of performance.

location modulation: See spatial* modulation.

loop: 1. A sequence of computer* instructions that is executed repeatedly until a specified condition is satisfied. 2. A closed path designed for the continuous flow of electrical current*. See tape* loop.

loudspeaker: A transducer* that converts electrical current* represent-ing audio* frequencies* into airborne sound waves.

low-pass filter: An electronic filter* that allows frequencies* below a given cutoff point to pass through while attenuating severely all frequencies above that point.

lujon: A percussion instrument made of six large metal squares that has a resonating quality similar to a vibraphone* or marimba in its lowest registers. Luciano Berio uses the mellow but characteristically vague sound of the lujon in his composition, *Circles* (1960).

Lydian minor scale: A synthetic* scale in which the lower tetrachord* has the same structure as the lower tetrachord of the Lydian mode and the upper tetrachord has the same structure as the upper tetrachord of the natural minor scale.

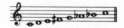

M

machine aesthetic: See mechanistic* aesthetic and futurism*.

machine language: An instruction code* consisting of symbols, characters, or signs that can be used directly, without translation, by a specific digital* computer. Instructions for the synthesis or composition of music by computer are usually set down in a specific program* which is then translated into machine language in an early stage of computer processing.

machine music: See mechanistic* aesthetic.

macrotonal scale: Any scale composed of intervals larger than whole tones.

mag: An abbreviation for magnetic or, in film* music, magnetic* track.

magic realism: A twentieth century style of painting in which objects are rendered with great precision and adherence to their natural state. The haunting quality of such works is accomplished through the juxtaposition of disparate time and space elements. Andrew Wyeth and Henry Koerner are American artists who have worked in this idiom.

magic square: A word arrangement in which the letters form the same words and result in the same meaning when considered either horizontally or vertically in either direction. The most famous magic square is an old Latin saying: "The sower Arepo keeps the work circling".

S A T O R
A R E P O
T E N E T
O P E R A
R O T A S

The same organizational logic is often employed in twelve-tone* technique. See palindrome*.

magnetic print-through: See print-through*.

magnetic tape: Metallic-oxide coated plastic tape used in magnetic recordings. Standard widths are one-quarter inch, one-half inch, and one inch. Magnetic tape is used in both audio* and video* tape* recording. See tape* recorder.

magnetic tape recording: See tape* recording.

magnetic track: A term used in film* music to refer to the portion of a 35MM film which is coated with metallic oxide and thus capable of accepting and storing audio* information. See tape* recorder, track*.

major Locrian scale: A synthetic* scale in which the lower tetrachord* has the same structure as the lower tetrachord of a major scale and the upper tetrachord has the same structure as the upper tetrachord of the Locrian mode.

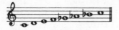

mambo: A Latin American dance very popular in the United States during the 1950's. The typical mambo is in 4/4 and accents the second and fourth pulses in the measure.

manual controller: A hand-operated device used to control electronic equipment. A potentiometer* is an example of a manual controller.

mapping: The employment of symbols (such as integers) to stand for pitches in the twelve-tone* system. See numerical* notation.

marimba eroica: A percussion instrument invented by composer Harry Partch that utilizes wooden planks as resonators mounted on nodes of foam rubber. The player stands on a platform fourteen inches high to perform on the instrument. The largest resonator is eight feet long, four feet high, and fourteen inches wide. The lowest tone is F below the lowest A on the piano, with the highest roughly equivalent to A an octave above the lowest A on the piano. The instrument is played with heavy mallets, and the performer wears padded gloves while performing.

Markoff chain music: 1. Zeroth-order: Computer* or other mathematically generated music in which each successive event* (note, interval, etc.) is arrived at in random fashion with no relationship to previous events. For example, it would be possible for a melody starting on G to progress to any other note governed only by established conditions of probability*. 2. First-order: Each successive event is dependent upon the immediately preceding event. 3. Second-order: Each successive event is dependent upon the preceding two events. 4. Third-order and above: Each successive event is dependent upon the preceding three or more events.

Markoff process: A mathematical process based on probability* theory in which each successive event is arrived at in random fashion with no relationship to previous events. Markoff process has been applied in the composition of computer* music, aleatoric* music, and computational* music. See Markoff* chain music.

Markov: See Markoff.

masking: The effect created when a tone blocks or makes inaudible a second tone that is weaker because of higher frequency* or less volume.

matrix: 1. Any table of items. 2. A network of circuit* elements such as transistors*, capacitors*, and relays* interconnected to perform a specific function in a computer*, synthesizer*, or other piece of electronic equipment. 3. A block or geometric pattern of numbers used to indicate relationships between elements of music such as pitch, duration, and dynamic level. See array*.

mechanistic aesthetic: An early twentieth-century glorification of the cold precision of machines in reaction to the sentimentality and emotional excesses of romanticism. A typical example of music of this genre is George Antheil's *Ballet Mécanique* (1923-1924) for nine pianos (including a player piano), four xylophones, large and small bells, gong, cymbal, woodblock, triangle, military drum, tambourine, tenor and bass drums, assorted electric door bells, and an airplane propeller sound. The composer noted that this work was written to "warn the age in which I was living of the simultaneous beauty and danger of its own unconscious mechanistic philosophy". Max Brand in his opera *Machinist Hopkins* (1929) and Arthur Honegger in *Pacific 231* (1924) also glorified the machine. See futurism*.

megahertz: A unit of frequency* equal to one million cycles* per second or one million hertz*.

mellophonium: An instrument developed for jazz* by Stan Kenton that looks much like a French horn with a straight bell. The sound of the instrument carries more directly than the standard French horn. The mellophonium has found its way into jazz as a solo instrument.

melochord: See Bode* melochord.

melodic prototype: The defining characteristics of a twelve-tone* row such as its motivic and rhythmic structure that are carried through in a composition in order to achieve musical continuity and coherence.

melodium: An early electronic instrument built by H. Bode in Berlin in 1938. See Bode* melochord.

memory: See storage*.

mese: A note of tonal or melodic importance located in the center of an array* of notes.

metamorphosis: The transformation of a previously stated musical figure or idea through modification of its basic form or structure. Motives, melodies, and themes are given new character and significance by changing their shapes and forms. Some of the processes used to alter a musical idea are inversion*, retrograde*, transposition*, variation, extension, fragmentation*, augmentation*, diminution*, and interval* variation.

metrical chord: Composer Henry Cowell's term for a variety of polymeter* based on numbers derived from the partials* of the harmonic* series. A tonal chord such as the triad C E G would, for example, generate the meters 2/4, 3/4, and 5/4 since the C represents the second partial of the fundamental C, G represents the third partial, and E the fifth partial. These meters would occur simultaneously in a composition.

metrical modulation: A transition from one meter or tempo to another through common note values or pulses that remain constant. Meter or tempo changes can be accomplished very smoothly and accurately by this process. The example below is derived from *Eight Etudes and a Fantasy for Woodwind Quartet* (1950) by Elliott Carter, who is generally considered to be the originator of metrical modulation:

metric modulation: See metrical* modulation.

mHz: Abbreviation for megahertz*.

microphone: A device that translates sound waves into fluctuating voltage* for purposes of amplification or recording. See tape* recorder, amplifier*.

microtonalism: The use of intervals of less than a semitone in musical composition. While not normal in older traditional music of the Western world, microtonal relationships are prevalent in music of other cultures, particularly those of Asia, as well as in contemporary music. Probably the most common microtone is the quarter-tone* which is a more or less exact split in half of the equal-tempered semitone. Alois Hába used both quarter and sixth-tone relationships. Other composers have used tones of less than a quarter-tone. Harry Partch has divided the octave into forty-three unequal steps and Julián Carrillo has divided it into ninety-six equal steps. The great freedom and variety of pitch relationships in electronic* music have given new impetus to microtonalism. While there is no standardized notation for microtonal music, Hába and Krzysztof Penderecki, among others, have developed usable systems.

middleground: A term employed by theorist Heinrich Schenker to indicate a "sketch" that would show important structural features of a composition, minus those details which are a part of the surface detail (e.g., embellishments, melodic ornamentation, arpeggiation, repetitions of certain notes, and/or note patterns). Important events* in the middleground would tend to gravitate around descending scale steps and the concept of chord prolongation*, in which one chord would govern an area of harmonic/melodic activity and subordinate other chords to its basic function. Schenker felt that the genius of a composer was revealed on the middleground level. See background*, foreground*, Schenkerian* analysis.

mike: See microphone*.

millimetration: A compositional process used by Heitor Villa-Lobos in which the outline of a photograph, map, chart, or drawing is put on graph paper and then translated into notation by assigning the vertical graph units corresponding pitches and the horizontal graph units note values. This technique was used by Villa-Lobos in *New York Skyline* (1940). See graph* notation.

minimal art: Artistic expression in which the simplest possible idea or gesture is employed. For example, a poem consisting of only a few words, a painting with only a single color, or a musical composition with only one or two notes. See anti-music*.

MIR: An acronym for Musical Information Retrieval, a computer* program* developed in 1964 at Princeton University by Arthur Mendel and Lewis Lockwood. MIR is intended primarily for the theoretical analysis and cataloging of existing musical compositions.

mirror: The most common use of this term is as a synonym for strict inversion*. In this context a motive, line, or chord is restated with the exact same interval structure, but progressing in the opposite vertical direction as though a mirror were held under the written notes. (See example a below.) A much less common use of this term is as a synonym for retrograde*. In this context the musical material is restated backwards beginning with the last note as though a mirror were placed at the end. (See example b below.)

mirror chord: See reflective* chord.

mirror inversion: See mirror*.

Mittelgrund: German for middleground*, as used in Schenkerian* analysis.

mixed-media art: See multimedia* art.

mixer: An electronic device used to combine incoming signals* and readjust their relative amplitudes* before routing them to other electronic instruments.

mixing: The process of combining signals*, readjusting their relative amplitudes*, and routing them to other electronic instruments.

mixturtrautonium: An electronic* musical instrument developed by Oscar Sala that was an improved and expanded form of the trautonium*. Sala wrote *Concertino for Mixturtrautonium and Electric Orchestra* in 1953.

modal interchange: Moving from one mode to another mode while the tonal center remains the same. For example, changing from E Dorian to E Phrygian. See modality*.

modality: The use of the church modes (Dorian, Phrygian, Lydian, etc.) of the Middle Ages as scale resources for musical compositions. See neomodality*.

modal modulation: The movement of a given mode from one tonal center to another. For example, changing from E Dorian to B Dorian. See modality*.

modern jazz: A term loosely attached to jazz* music after ca. 1950. Included under this heading would be categories such as cool* jazz, bossa* nova, progressive* jazz, third* stream music and new* wave jazz.

modifier: A generic term used to identify any electronic device that changes a characteristic or characteristics of a signal*. See filter*, modulator*, reverberation* unit, amplifier*.

modular electronic system: An electronic equipment network such as a synthesizer* in which individual instruments or units of circuitry (modules) can be readily added or removed.

modulation (electronic): The use of one waveform* to alter a characteristic of another waveform so that it corresponds to the pattern of the modulating waveform. See modulator*, amplitude* modulation, frequency* modulation, ring* modulator.

original waveform	ᴶᴸᴸᴸᴸᴸᴸᴸᴸᴸ
modulating waveform	‿‿‿
resultant waveform	ᴶᴸᴸᴸᴸᴸᴸ

modulator: An electronic instrument that produces a signal* used to alter the characteristics of another signal. The signal from the modulator causes the other signal to respond in the pattern of the modulating signal. See modulation*.

module: An individual instrument or unit of circuitry that can readily be added to or removed from an electronic equipment network such as a synthesizer*.

monad: A one-note structural unit in music.

monaural: Sound reproduction involving only one channel* as opposed to stereophonic* sound which involves two or more channels and creates a new sound dimension — that of spatial orientation.

monitor head: See playback* head.

monodrama: A work written for the stage which employs only one actor, singer or speaker. Arnold Schoen-. berg's *Erwartung* written in 1909 is in this form.

monophonic sound: A sound system that reproduces sound on one channel* from one or more input* signals*. See monaural*.

Moog synthesizer: An electronic* music synthesizer* manufactured by R. A. Moog, Inc., in which modules* are interconnected primarily by patch* chords. Sound production and modification in this synthesizer are primarily activated by voltages* generated by a linear* controller, a keyboard* controller and a sequential* controller.

montage: A technique common to the visual arts in which a number of elements or items of similar nature are assembled into a composite. In films, montage denotes the selection, cutting, and splicing together of separate shots. When used in a musical context, the term usually refers to the overall effect created by the juxtaposition and overlapping of various more or less heterogeneous musical elements. Montage is an important concept in electronic* music. See collage*.

Monte Carlo method: An experimental technique that employs random sampling, trial-and-error, and probability* to arrive at solutions to problems. This statistical process is often used in computer* operations and aleatoric* composition.

morphology: 1. Of a sound: the form of a sound—how it begins, continues and ends. See envelope*. 2. Of a composition: the overall structure of a work as a composite of textures, dynamics, timbres, etc.

morphophone: An electronic device used by composers of musique* concrète, particularly the group associated with the French* National Radio in the 1950's. It is a closed*

loop tape* playback* device with ten playback* heads each connected to a separate preamplifier*. Through the circuitry of the morphophone artificial reverberation* and timbre* can be superimposed on existing sounds.

motown: A general term used to identify a kind of black rhythm* and blues music emanating from Detroit, Michigan. Motown features a light, evenly-stressed beat, basic blues* progressions, parallel chordal movement (e.g., I-II-III-IV-III-II-I), and simple melodic lines often accompanied by a type of gospel* hand-clapping or foot-stomping. A typical motown group has a lead singer backed up by a small group of voices who serve as a rhythmic foil for the lead. The background voices often enunciate nonsense lyrics such as continuous "uh-huhs" or "shoob-doop-be-doops." Some well-known motown groups include the Marvelettes, the Miracles, the Vandellas, and the Supremes. Motown is also the business title of the recording company that produces and markets this music.

moviola: An item of equipment used in writing and editing film* music through which the motion picture can be viewed while two or three sound* tracks can be heard simultaneously. The film can be run fast, slow, or even a single frame at a time. The moviola is used for the synchronization of sound and picture.

multidimensional musical space: A theory attributed to Arnold Schoenberg in which the twelve-tone* row, regardless of the way it is modified by the composer in the course of the composition, always retains its basic identity. Supposedly, the listener always perceives the essential character of the row, regardless of the permutations* it undergoes.

multimedia art: Creative expression

which employs two or more art forms. The most commonly combined elements are music, the visual arts (including film), dance, and theatre. Some examples are *No Dead Horses on the Moon* (1969) by Allen Strange, involving film projectors and recorded sound; *The Maze* (1967) by Larry Austin, involving the audience, lighting effects, and performers who are also actors; and *Third Planet from the Sun* (1969) by Ramon Zupko, which includes electronic sounds, recorded voices, actors doing pantomime, dancers, a chorus that speaks, sings and acts, instrumentalists, films, and lighting effects including strobe lights and a color* organ.

multimeter: Frequent metric changes in quick succession, such as two measures of 3/4 followed by five measures of 5/8 followed by three measures of 2/4, etc. Some writers (e.g., Gardner Read) use the term variable* meter to indicate multimeter.

multi-octave scale: See two-octave* scale.

multiphonic: A term coined by the writer Bruno Bartolozzi to denote multiple sounds produced simultaneously on a woodwind instrument. A multiphonic sound is created by the predominance of certain partials. Particular fingerings will divide an air column into segments, especially if an open key corresponds to a node of a fundamental*. Tonal color is thus modified according to which partials are subdued and which are enhanced. Lip pressure, mouthpiece design, and the idiosyncrasies of a particular instrument will determine the success of multiphonic sounds. A similar technique on brass instruments involves humming and playing at the same time.

multiple tonality: See polytonality*.

multiple-track tape recorder: A tape* recorder capable of recording or playing back three or more channels* of information simultaneously. This kind of machine is used commercially to combine a number of channels into two channels for standard stereo* playback*, and used in electronic* music studios to record a number of channels independently and then combine them in a synchronized manner with previously recorded materials. Generally, three-track and four-track* machines of this type use one-half inch wide magnetic* tape. Eight-track and twelve-track machines use one inch tape and sixteen-track and twenty-four-track machines use two inch tape.

multi-track tape machine: See multiple-track* tape recorder.

multi-vibrator: An oscillator* used for the generation of square* waves. See electronic* music.

MUSIC: A program* developed by Max Matthews at Bell* Laboratories which can be used to synthesize sound by computer*.

musical gesture: The expression of a musical idea which can range from a significant group of a few notes to an entire piece.

musical graphics: See graphic* notation.

MUSICOMP: An abbreviation for Music Simulator-Interpreter for Composition Procedures, a computer* program* developed by Lejaren Hiller and Robert Baker at the University of Illinois and used by them to compose *Computer Cantata* in 1963. MUSICOMP was later used by Hiller and John Cage in the creation of *HPSCHD* (1969).

musique concrète: One of the earliest forms of electronic* music in which basic sound sources were other than traditionally employed musical instruments and voices, or electronically generated sounds. It grew out of experimentation by Pierre Schaeffer and his colleagues at French* National Radio in Paris in 1948 and established the concept that any aural sensation was viable raw material for creative endeavor. All kinds of natural and man-made sounds were employed, including those made by crowds, automobiles, machines, animals, the speaking voice, and percussion instruments. The basic sound materials were recorded and subjected to various forms of tape* manipulation (speed change, direction change, reverberation*, editing, etc.). Musique concrète seems to have been more important as a forerunner of electronic* music than as a significant art form in its own right. Edgar Varèse's *Déserts* (1954) and *Poème électronique* (1958) stand as the only generally recognized masterpieces using musique concrète techniques.

MUSTUD: A group of computer* programs* developed by Gerald Lefkoff for use in the analysis of musical style.

mutation: An altered form of a scale, motive, theme, or twelve-tone* row.

Muzak: Recorded background music piped into public establishments such as supermarkets, banks, air terminals, or medical offices via special telephone circuits. Early work was done by George Squire in 1911 in this field, but it was not until the 1950's that the system was fully developed. By 1957 it was calculated that 75,000,000 Americans were exposed to muzak during some portion of the day. Muzak is designed to create certain types of moods by stressing light novelty tunes during the breakfast hour, ballads with lots of strings during lunch and the early afternoon hours, and up-tempo "businessman's bounce" arrangements* during the early evening hours when many people feel tired and psychologically fatigued. Typical Muzak programs are made to comprise a twenty-four

hour sequence broken into three eight-hour reels. Muzak is calculated not to be listened to (!) in the sense that it should not be intrusive in any way upon the aural psyche of the listener.

mystic chord: A chord created by Alexander Scriabin, a composer who was constantly striving for enigmatic and complex harmonic structures in his music. The mystic chord is also referred to as the Prometheus chord as it was first used in Scriabin's composition of that name written in 1910.

N

N⁻: Symbol for Nebenstimme*.

nail pizzicato: A string technique developed by Béla Bartók in which the string is plucked with the fingernail, creating a snapping sound. The notational symbol for the nail pizzicato is a circle with a dot in the center placed over the note, as in the example below.

NC: Abbreviation for note cancrizans* —a retrograde* of the note series*.

neapolitan major scale: A synthetic* scale consisting of seven notes. Its unique feature is that its inversion* is also its retrograde*. The name of the scale is derived from the half-step relationship between the first and second degree which can be found in the traditional neapolitan sixth chord.

neapolitan minor scale: A synthetic* scale consisting of seven notes. This scale is similar to the neapolitan* major scale except that a half step exists between the fifth and sixth degrees of the scale

Nebenstimme: The subordinate or secondary line or motive in a musical composition. Arnold Schoenberg used the symbol for Nebenstimme (N⌐) along with the symbol for Hauptstimme* (H⌐) in the scores and parts of his works in order to aid the performer in perceiving salient and/ or subsidiary passages in contrapuntal textures. Alban Berg used both H⌐ and N⌐ in his works as well, and both men felt that these signs would aid their listeners in the act of musical comprehension. The sign ⌐ indicated that the marked passage had come to a close.

neo-classicism: A style of musical composition that emerged in the early 1920's as a reaction against romanticism, impressionism*, and atonality*. Neo-classicism was characterized by a return to the spirit, forms, techniques, and ideals of seventeenth and eighteenth century music. Some composers emulated the order, balanced forms, and objectivism of Haydn and Mozart, while others employed the forms and contrapuntal techniques of J.S. Bach (sometimes referred to as neo-baroque). A renewed interest in the harpsichord, a non-programmatic orientation to music, and a special interest in contrapuntal forms such as the canon and fugue were further manifestations of neo-classicism. Composers associated with this movement at one time or another include Igor Stravinsky (usually thought of as the founder of neo-classicism), Béla Bartók, Ernest Bloch, Paul Hindemith and Sergei Prokofiev.

neo-impressionism: A branch of post-impressionism* that developed in the last two decades of the 19th century as a reaction against impressionism*. In painting, such artists as Seurat and Signac applied pure colors in small dots which would then fuse through optical mixture when viewed from a distance creating other hues. (For example, the intermingling of small yellow and blue dots would appear as green.) This style of painting was based on scientific optical theories as opposed to the subjective approach to color in impressionism. The terms pointillism* and divisionism are often used interchangeably with neo-impressionism. Pointillistic orchestration can be found in Anton Webern's *Six Orchestral Pieces* (1913) and *Cantata*, Op. 29 (1940), where pure instrumental colors are intermingled, paralleling the ideology and techniques of the neo-impressionist painters.

neo-modality: The use of modal scales and hamonies in a contemporary musical work. Composers such as Béla Bartók (who studied modal folk music in countries such as Hungary, Rumania, and Transylvania and incorporated this material into works of his own such as *Mikrokosmos* [1926-37]), Jean Sibelius (*Symphony No. 4* [1911]), Aaron Copland (*Violin Sonata* [1943]), Roy Harris (*American Ballads* [1947]), and Randall Thompson (*String Quartet No. 1* [1941]), re-examined the potential of modal material for creating a variety of sound unhampered by some of the limitations found in the diatonic major and minor scales. Rock* musicians have also used modal melodies and harmonic progressions quite effectively. They often employ parallel modal harmonic patterns and avoid the traditional flavor of the authentic cadence via the use of the phrygian cadence and the non-leading tone effect of ♭VII-I. See modality*.

neophonic orchestra: An enlarged jazz* band that contains such instruments as tuba, flute, alto flute, bassoon, oboe, bass clarinet, and an enlarged percussion section in adition to the more usual instruments such as trumpets, trombones, saxophones and percussion. Bandleader Stan Kenton introduced The Los Angeles Neophonic Orchestra in 1965, starting the concept that later became popular on college campuses across the nation.

neo-romanticism: An art movement of the second quarter of the twentieth century which was a reaction against the objective, scientific, and analytical styles of post-impressionism*, cubism*, fauvism*, and neo-classicism*. The political and economic upheaval of the times fostered a return to the earlier concepts of humanism, emotion, sentiment, and mood. Painters identified with this movement were Berman, Berard, and Tchelitchew. In music there was a parallel revival of dramatic, poetic, and programmatic music with a resurgence of melody of a more vocal nature. Among the compositions that can be classified as neo-romantic are Béla Bartók's *Concerto for Orchestra* (1944) and Paul Hindemith's *Mathis der Maler* (1938). Composers who write or have written mainly in this vein are Carl Orff, William Walton, Virgil Thomson, Howard Hanson, and Samuel Barber.

nesting: The use of unordered intersections* where set* segments* or adjacencies* interact in two or more permutations* of a set.

neue Musik: German for new* music.

neutral triad: Theorist Joseph Yasser's term for a chord of three tones containing two equal thirds which together comprise the interval of a perfect fifth.

new music: A general term that includes many of the musical idioms and techniques of the twentieth century, such as atonalism*, serialism*, modality*, aleatory*, and elec-

tronic* music. The term first became popular during the 1920's and is somewhat obsolete today. In some circles the term is used synonymously with avant-garde*.

New Orleans style: Jazz* as played by artists such as Joe "King" Oliver, Ferdinand "Jelly Roll" Morton and their bands in Storyville in the early decades of the twentieth century. The typical New Orleans jazz combo* consisted of five or six players, most often including trumpet, trombone, clarinet, piano, bass, and drums. New Orleans style was highly improvisatory as the great majority of musicians could not read music. It is difficult to describe the sound of this early music accurately since there are few recordings available prior to 1923. The blues*, popular ballads, stomps, marches, and spirituals* were all used as basic materials for improvisation. Ragtime* was also a primary influence in developing the relaxed, polyphonically intricate, and collective improvisational feeling of New Orleans style. The musicians tended to stay fairly close to the melody during improvisation and favored arpeggiated figures along with growls* and the frequent use of blue* notes. Other important musicians include Louis Armstrong, Leon Roppolo, Sidney Bechet, Edward "Kid" Ory, Sam Morgan, and Bunk Johnson.

new wave: A term often applied to the jazz* music of musicians such as John Coltrane, Don Cherry, Ornette Coleman, Charles Taylor, Charlie Mingus, and Eric Dolphy, in which a certain freedom is attained through the avoidance of traditional jazz chord patterns and forms as the source of framework for improvisation*. Instead, the focus is placed upon melody and melodic inflection, including a rather extensive use of microtones*. In addition, modifications are often made to the instruments in order to achieve new means for sound production. The new wave movement began in the early 1960's.

NI: Abbreviation for inversion* of the note series*.

ninth chord: A vertical* sonority consisting of a combination of a triad and the intervals of a seventh and a ninth above the triad's root. The triad and the two intervals can vary in quality.

noiseband: A limited area of random frequencies* usually derived by processing white* noise through a band-pass* filter.

noise generator: See white* noise generator.

noise music: See futurism*.

nonad: A vertical* sonority consisting of nine different pitches not counting octave doublings.

non-combinatorial: A twelve-tone* row or set* that does not possess the property of combinatoriality*.

non-objective art: Any non-representational aspect or trend in modern art. See abstract* expressionism, action* painting.

non-periodic: This term pertains to vibrations or other phenomena that do not recur at regular intervals.

non-retrogradable rhythm: A pattern of durations that reads the same backward or forward.

non-tertial harmony: See non-tertian* harmony.

non-tertian harmony: Chords constructed in intervals other than thirds.

non-triadic tonality: The gravitation of a group of pitches around a central pitch that occurs without the harmonic and intervallic relationships normally associated with traditional tonality. See polarity*.

notch filter: See band-elimination* filter.

note class: See pitch* class.

note complex: Any combination of notes sounded simultaneously. This term is used synonymously with vertical* sonority and simultaneity* by many contemporary musicians to replace the traditional term "chord" which to many connotes a traditional structure in thirds.

note-density: The distribution of single notes and chords within a composition. A musical texture consisting of many simultaneous sounds would have a high level of note-density.

note field: An unordered group of of notes that is treated more or less as a unit in chance* music.

note mixture: 1. In instrumental music: an attack* followed by a long reverberation* (as with bells, drums or chimes). 2. In electronic* music: sinus* tone mixtures in which the frequencies* of the partials* are not ordered harmonically (i.e., they cannot be expressed by simple numerical proportions). See harmonic*.

note qualities: A term used by Hungarian composer György Ligeti and others as a synonym for pitch° classes.

novachord: An early electronic* musical instrument with a single keyboard which is capable of producing individual pitches, chords, and percussion effects with variable sound envelopes*. The novachord is similar in operation to the solovox*.

NS: Abbreviation for note series*, which is synonymous with original° or prime*.

numerical notation: The assignment of integers to represent notes in a twelve-tone* row. See order* number, pitch* number, order-number* pitch-number couple.

O

O: Abbreviation for original*.

Oberheim music modulator: An electronic* music system based on the ring* modulation principle that may be used for either live performances or laboratory-generated sounds. The modulator* includes a preamplifier*, an adjustable sine* wave oscillator*, a balanced modulator, and a microphone*.

objectivism: A general term used to describe art that treats events, objects, or phenomena with as little distortion as possible created by the artist's personal feelings or reflections.

oboic flux: A modern technique for the harp in which a glissando is performed near the sounding board. The term was coined by the composer/harpist Carlos Salzedo. The oboic flux is indicated in the following manner:

octad: A vertical* sonority consisting of eight different pitches not counting octave doublings.

octatonic scale: An eight-note scale in which half and whole steps alternate. Igor Stravinsky used the octatonic scale in *Noces*. (1922).

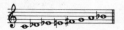

octave equivalence: 1. In tonal music: the concept that notes at the intervallic relationship of an octave (or multiples of an octave) have the same harmonic function. **2.** In twelve-tone* technique: the concept that notes at the intervallic relationship of an octave (or multiples of an octave) hold the same position in the twelve-tone* row. See pitch* class.

off note: A pitch that deviates slightly from the norm, found commonly in jazz*. Off notes are usually blue* notes, or they fluctuate as a kind of "between the keys" effect as played on a wind instrument. See blue* note.

omni-directional: A microphone* that picks up sound from all directions, as opposed to a uni-directional* microphone.

Once Group: A Michigan-based group of avant-garde* composers organized in the 1960's for the purpose of presenting performances of new music. Some composers who have been associated with this group are Robert Ashley, Gordon Mumma, and George Cacioppo.

ondes martenot: An electronic* musical instrument invented by the Frenchman Maurice Martenot in the late 1920's. Basic sound production is of the beat-frequency type similar to that of the theremin*. The ondes martenot has two controllers*: a seven octave keyboard and a ribbon* which runs the length of the keyboard. The ribbon is used to produce varying pitches and vibrato by moving the index finger across it from left to right. After amplification the basic signal* of the ondes martenot is filtered* and then transmitted to a loudspeaker*. Some of the loudspeakers used have strings and a sounding board which add an eerie resonance to the sound. This instrument was used by Arthur Honegger in *Joan of Arc at the Stake* (1938) and by André Joilet in *A Concerto for Ondes Martenot and Orchestra,* first performed in Boston in 1950.

ondes musicales: See ondes* martenot.

one interval set: A twelve-tone* row created by repeating the same interval over and over. For example, a one interval set consisting only of perfect fifths (or, by means of the principle of octave* equivalence, perfect fourths).

oom-pah figuration: A type of accompaniment figure common to jazz* piano styles.

op art: Optical art (for which op art is a common diminutive) takes its impetus from the effects created by abstraction and optical illusion. Primary in the mind of the op artist is the interplay between the viewer and the work. Here, more than perhaps in most other kinds of art, the viewer must physically interact with the illusion of movement or depth created by the work. Typical works in this style explore optical phenomena through the employment of geometrical patterns and designs of bright colors that often appear to move or change as the viewer beholds the canvas. This movement first appeared in New York City around 1963. Some notable op artists include Bridget Riley, Frank Stella, Larry Poons, and Yaacow Agam.

open chord: A chord having an open or hollow sound, such as one built in perfect fourths or perfect fifths. This term is not to be confused with the techniques of open and closed position common to traditional music theory.

open reel: A standard tape* reel, as opposed to a cassette*.

operation: 1. A general term borrowed from mathematics, usually used to encompass all of the permutational* techniques in twelve-tone* music such as retrograde*, inversion*, etc. 2. A procedure in the composition or performance of chance* or electronic* music. 3. A function of a computer* or a computer program*.

operation code: See order* code.

optical painting: See op* art.

optical scanner: A device that reads material printed in special magnetic ink and relays the data to a computer*.

optical siren: An electronic device consisting of a revolving disk, a photoelectric cell, and a beam of light used in the composition of electronic* music. Designs are cut in paper which in turn is placed on the revolving disk. As the disk interrupts the light beam, current* variations are produced via the photoelectric cell. This varying current is then converted into sound by other electronic devices.

optical track: A term used in film* music to refer to the portion of a 35MM film which is used to store audio* information by means of patterns of light that are translated into sound by a photoelectric cell. See magnetic* track.

order code: The part of a computer* program* that represents a specific operation to be performed. For example, AD would instruct the computer to add numbers and SU would instruct it to subtract.

ordered pitch classes: A collection of three or more notes in a twelve-tone* work in which each note is from a different pitch* class and there is a specified succession. For example, the occurence of E, Bb, and F in exactly that sequence at various times in a composition. See unordered* pitch classes, ordered* set.

ordered set: A collection of notes (usually in the form of a twelve-tone* row) in which a specified succession is a defining characteristic. See set*, unordered* set.

order number: A number assigned to a note in a twelve-tone* row that indicates the position of the note in the prime* form of the row. The integers 0 to 11 are generally used.

order-number pitch-number couple: A numerical designation that identifies precisely a note in a twelve-tone* row. The first number indicates the position of the note in the row, the second indicates the number of half steps that particular note lies above the initial note of the original* form of the row regardless of octave register. For this purpose the numbers 0 to 11 are employed. The order-number pitch-number couples are shown below for Schoenberg's *Piano Suite*, Op. 25 (1924). See order* number, pitch* number.

(0,0) (1,1) (2,3) (3,9) (4,2) (5,11) (6,4) (7,10) (8,7) (9,8) (10,5) (11,6)

organic scale: Theorist Joseph Yasser's term for a scale that develops according to inherent "organic" laws of musical consciousness and is found the world over. The pentatonic* and diatonic scales would fall into this category, and Yasser states that his supradiatonic* scales will become another scale of this order.

oriental scale: A synthetic* scale stemming from music of Eastern cultures that consists of seven notes arranged in the following interval pattern:

original: See prime*.

original primitive: A term from the Schillinger* system used to denote scales found in primitive music in their original form (usually containing seven pitches or less) modified to equal temperament tuning for use in the context of Western music.

oscillator: An electronic device that produces one or more repetitive waveforms* at a specific frequency*. See square* wave, sine* wave, pulse* wave, sawtooth* wave, triangular* wave, electronic* music, voltage* controlled oscillator.

oscillograph: The visual display of an electronic signal* on the screen of an oscilloscope*.

oscilloscope: An electronic device that reproduces the waveform* of a signal* on a fluorescent screen of a cathode-ray tube. The oscilloscope is used to study visually sound characteristics such as frequency*, amplitude*, and harmonics*.

oscilloscopic art: A form of multimedia* artistic expression concerned with the production and manipulation of Lissajous* figures on oscilloscope screens or television sets by means of audio* signals*. Composer Lowell Cross, among others, has been experimenting with this combination of aural and visual experiences since the mid-1960's.

ostinato: A repeated rhythmic/melodic phrase unit, usually found in the bass and extended over considerable time spans in a composition. Although the ostinato stems from music prior to the twentieth century, it has found a real home in contemporary music because of its inherent ability to unify musical material. The first example (on the following page) is an ostinato found in the cello part of Béla Bartók's *String Quartet No. 6* (1939) (first movement). The second example, from Igor Stravinsky's *Sonata for Two Pianos* (1944) illustrates a more chordal type of ostinato.

OT: An abbreviation used to indicate a transposed original* form of a twelve-tone* row.

out-chorus: The final ensemble section in a jazz* performance, noted for its climactic, loud and exuberant spirit.

output: 1. Electrical energy or information in other forms that is produced by an electronic circuit* or device. 2. The mechanical connection through which information leaves an electronic system. 3. Information that results from computer* processing.

overblowing: The ability to sound harmonics* above the fundamental* by controlling the breath on woodwind or brass instruments. See multiphonic*.

overlap: The process of smoothly connecting two musical segments in film* music by beginning the second segment while the first is dying away.

overlay: In film* music this term refers to a segment of music that is recorded over the original music track* in order to create a special effect.

overtone: An individual pure tone that is a component of a complex* tone and higher in pitch than the fundamental*. See harmonic*, partial*.

overtone scale: A synthetic* scale consisting of the eighth through fourteenth partials* of the harmonic* series.

overtone series: See harmonic* series.

P

P: Abbreviation for prime*.

palindrome: Something that reads the same backward or forward. An example of a word palindrome is "Otto". An example of a sentence palindrome is "Able was I ere I saw Elba". Musical lines, rhythm patterns, chord progressions and entire movements have been written in this manner. Paul Hindemith's *Fugue in F* from *Ludus Tonalis* (1943) is an example of a musical palindrome, as are all retrograde* canons. See magic* square.

panchromaticism: A term that refers to the unrestricted use of all twelve tones of the chromatic scale.

panchromatic chord: A simultaneously sounded group of notes that includes all or most of the twelve pitches of the chromatic scale. See tone* cluster.

pandiatonicism: The use of all of the pitches of a diatonic scale in either a cluster (e.g., the white keys on the piano) or melodically in a free fashion without the restrictions imposed by the functions of traditional tonality (e.g., leading-tone moving to or from tonic). Although the technique may be employed with a diatonic scale in any key, C major has been used most frequently because of its obvious accessibility. Pandiatonic harmony is usually rather static sounding due to the lack of pitches with operative functional relationships. Pandiatonic passages often employ ostinati*, contrapuntal movement in the upper registers, and a general lack of definitive cadence. Composers who have used this technique in their works include Roy Harris, Henry Cowell, William Schuman, Igor Stravinsky, and Aaron Copland.

panning: A technique used in electronic* music composition in which the sound image is made to move

progressively from one loudspeaker*
to another. See spatial* modulation.

panrhythm: A term coined by theorist
Rudolph Reti that denotes the use
of smaller metric units to form
larger metric designs. Hence, a
meter such as 11/8 might be comprised of units such as $\frac{2+3+4+2}{8}$.
Béla Bartók often uses such metric
groupings in his *Mikrokosmos* (1926-
37). An example of $\frac{3+2+3}{8}$ may be
seen in No. 151, Vol. VI. See additive* meter.

pantonality: Arnold Schoenberg preferred this term to · atonality* and
regarded pantonality as a synthesis
of tonalities rather than an actual
combination of all tonalities in a
given work. The term has come to
be synonymous with atonality.

paper flyspeck: A natural point of imperfection present in a sheet of
transparent paper. Aleatoric* composers such as John Cage have randomly arrived at pitches by tracing
these pointal imperfections onto
manuscript paper, creating notes
wherever they fall within or near a
staff.

paper-tape programmer: A device used
to encode information on paper tape
by punching patterns of holes that
can be interpreted by a computer*
or synthesizer*.

paper-tape reader: A device that converts information in the form of
perforation patterns on tape into a
set of electrical impulses* for use
by a computer*, synthesizer*, or
other electronic system.

parallel harmony: The successive movement of a chord structure to different pitch levels. Most often the sequence of pitch levels follows a
scale pattern. This method of orga-
nizing harmonies was employed frequently in impressionistic music as
it tends to negate the traditional
functions of chord progression with-

in tonality. Twentieth century music
from Claude Debussy, Béla Bartók,
and Igor Stravinsky to jazz* and
rock* abound in parallel harmony.
The term planing is used synonymously with parallel harmony. See
impressionism*. The following illustration of parallel harmony is from
Petrushka (1911) by Igor Stravinsky:

parallelism: The simultaneous movement of musical lines or chords
(see parallel* harmony) at the same
interval.

parameter: A term borrowed from
mathematics that describes a given
variable in music. Hence one may
speak of the parameter of pitch, texture, harmony, etc.

partial: An individual pure tone that
is a component of a complex* tone.
This term is similar in meaning to
harmonic*, but unlike harmonic can
be applied to noise sounds whose
component frequencies* do not coincide with the natural harmonic
series.

partial tone: See partial*.

partition: A term borrowed from mathematics, often used in conjunction
with twelve-tone* music, that denotes a division or sectionalization
of a tone* row as used in a particular piece. See segmentation.*

partituraphon: An early electronic*
musical instrument built by Jörg
Mager and introduced in 1935. The
partituraphon was a development of
Mager's earlier sphärophon* and
could perform any keyboard music.
It was used in theatrical productions
of its day until its destruction during World War II.

passive resolution: The dissipation of a dissonance through the retention of the dissonant note or notes while the remainder of the chord changes. In the example below the B♭ in the first chord receives a passive resolution in the second chord.

patch bay: See patch* panel.

patch cord: A section of electrical cable with a plug on each end used to connect jacks* on a patch* panel and thus complete an electronic circuit*.

patch panel: An array of jacks* used to interconnect the various components of an electronic system such as a synthesizer* through the use of patch* cords.

PC: Abbreviation for pitch* class.

peak: 1. The maximum amplitude* of a waveform*. 2. The highest voltage* level reached in a specific cycle or operation.

peak music power: The total amount of power that can be sent by an amplifier* into a speaker at one time.

pelog scale: A five-tone (pentatonic*) scale derived from Javanese music which has the following interval pattern:

pentachord: A scale or twelve-tone* row segment consisting of five notes.

pentad: A vertical* sonority consisting of five different pitches, not counting octave doublings.

pentatonic scale: Any scale containing five tones to the octave. One easily-remembered form can be found on the five black keys of the piano beginning on C sharp. Pentatonic scales are found indigenously in the music of the Far East, Polynesia, and Africa, but also occur in Western music (e.g., Irish and Scottish folk songs, music of the American Indian). Composers such as Igor Stravinsky, Béla Bartók, Claude Debussy, Gustav Mahler, and Paul Hindemith have found the scales useful in their compositions. See pelog* scale, kumoi* scale, hirajoshi* scale.

periodicity: The phenomenon of regular recurrence. Pitch results from frequency* periodicity.

permutation: 1. The changing in some specific way of the order of pitches in a twelve-tone* row. This can be accomplished by beginning the row on a note other than its first pitch, by the inversion*, retrograde* or retrograde-inversion* of the row, or by reordering the row through some other consistent method. 2. Any specific ordering of a twelve-tone* row may be viewed as a permutation of the twelve-note chromatic scale.

perpetual variation: A style of composition in which structural repetition of any kind is avoided and replaced by a continuous transformation of musical material.

phase: This term has been employed by Karlheinz Stockhausen and others to indicate the time-interval between impulses* that constitute sound. Phases may be periodic or aperiodic and can be classified into two groups — durations and pitches. A phase of 1/16 second or more between impulses is perceptible to the human ear and thus can be classified as a duration. In traditional music such aspects as rhythm and meter occur in the phase-duration* region of from 1/16 second to six seconds or more. A phase of 1/32 of a second or less between impulses is not perceptible to the ear and the alternation of impulses and phases of this short time-span creates a frequency* which results in pitch. The ear needs at least two equal phase-durations to recognize a pitch. The melodic and harmonic aspects of music occur in a phase-duration region of from approximately 1/32 second to 1/3200 second.

phase-duration: The length of time-interval (phase*) between the impulses* that constitute a sound.

Phasendauer: German for phase-duration*.

phon: A measuring unit for the loudness level of sound. Zero on the phon scale represents the faintest possible audible sound.

phoneme: The smallest unit of speech sound. Classes of phonemes are represented by phonetic symbols. For example, "c" as in "case" and "k" as in "kettle" are both represented as "k". In Kenneth Gaburo's *Antiphony IV* (1967) the text is broken into separate phonemes rather than occurring in the larger unit of syllables. See phonology*.

phonogene: An electronic device designed by Pierre Schaeffer which is used to process sounds in musique* concrète. With this equipment the complete sound spectrum of previously tape-recorded material (noises, vocal sounds, pitches, rhythmic patterns, etc.) can be transposed to twelve different pitch levels simultaneously. These pitch levels correspond to the twelve semitones in the equal tempered scale. The transpositions* are accomplished through the varying of tape speed. A twelve-key piano keyboard is used as a control. See morphophone*, tape* recorder.

phonology: The science of speech sounds. Many composers have studied phonology and applied its principles in works involved with text. For example, Kenneth Gaburo in *Antiphony IV* (1967) breaks the text into phonemes* which are tape* recorded and then manipulated in various ways.

PI: Abbreviation for point* of inversion.

pink noise: A pitchless, nonrepetitive signal* containing all audible frequencies* with an increase in relative amplitude* of the lower frequencies. See white* noise, blue* noise.

pink sound: See pink* noise.

pitch class: A term coined by composer and theorist Milton Babbitt and used especially by writers of serial* music to denote the octave* equivalence of the pitches in the equal-tempered system. Hence, there are twelve different pitch classes (all C's are one pitch class, all C♯'s another pitch class, etc.). The term also recognizes the enharmonic identity of pitches (e.g., B♯ is equivalent in pitch class to C).

pitch field: All of the pitches found in either an entire composition or some part thereof.

pitch number: A number assigned to a note in a twelve-tone* row (see example a) that indicates the place of that note in the ascending chromatic scale of the first note of the prime* form of the row (see example b). The integers* 0 to 11 are generally used. After pitch numbers have been assigned they can be arranged so that they represent the original* row (see example c). See order* number, pitch-number* order-number couple, interval-vector*.

pitch-time event: This term is used synonymously with pitch, tone, and sometimes event*.

planing: See parallel* harmony.

playback: Reproducing for the listener, sound on magnetic* tape, phonograph record, or film.

playback head: The part of a tape recorder that translates magnetic patterns on tape* into fluctuating voltage*. See tape* recorder, erase* head, record* head.

plunger: A rubber toilet plunger often used by brass players in jazz* ensembles for muting effects.

pointal imperfection: See paper* flyspeck.

pointillism: A branch of French impressionism* in which tiny dots of color are applied to the canvas creating recognizable images when the eye mixes the colors at a distance. The chief exponent of pointillism was Georges Seurat (1859-1891). His painting *A Sunday Afternoon on the Island of La Grande Jatte* is perhaps the most famous example of this technique. Other pointillists include Paul Signac, Camille Pissaro and Vincent Van Gogh. In music the term has been adopted to apply to textures in which a rarified atmosphere prevails, governed by fragmented voices, disjunct melodic lines, frequent rests, and emphasis on dynamics, accent, and tone color. Anton Webern is the composer usually identified most readily with this musical style. See Klangfarbenmelodie*.

point of inversion: The interval found at the point where two hexachords* of a set* divide when the second hexachord is an inversion of the first one. In combinatorial* situations the intervals of a minor second, minor third, perfect fourth, perfect fifth, major sixth, or major seventh are used as the point of inversion.

polarity: Composer Igor Stravinsky in his book *Poetics of Music* (1948) uses this term to describe the attraction of a tone, an interval or a complex of tones towards a given point. Polarity is a more general term than tonality, which is usually viewed within the major-minor framework. See centric* priority.

polinome: An electronic device used in performance situations where different tempi are being utilized simultaneously. A control panel regulates metronomic speed which is heard by the performers through headphones*, or it can regulate flashing lights to convey metronomic speed to the performers if headphones are impractical. Emmanual Ghent is credited as being the inventor of this device. See coordinome*.

polychord: A vertical* sonority consisting of two or more identifiable chord structures such as triads or seventh chords.

polycluster: Tone* clusters of different intervallic construction (such as one built in minor seconds, another in major and minor seconds, another in whole tones) that are used simultaneously in a composition. In order to facilitate their individuality as harmonic units they are often placed in different registers or set apart through orchestration.

polyharmony: See polychord*.

polymeter: The juxtaposition of two or more different metric schemes in a composition. Usually the different meters will have a common beat, unit, or subdivision. Theoretically, the term polymeter should be reserved for those situations in which three or more different meters are aligned, and bimeter* should be employed to designate those situations in which only two different meters are combined. When different meters are aligned, the contrasting patterns of stress emphasis will produce cross-accents. (See example a.) Some works containing polymeter include Benjamin Britten's *War Requiem* (1962), Charles Ives' *Three Places in New England* (1935), Igor Stravinsky's *Histoire du Soldat* (1918), Paul Hindemith's *Mathis der Maler* (1938), and Béla Bartók's *String Quartet No. 3* (1927). In the Bartók quartet both parts are indicated in the same meter (i.e., 3/4) at one point, even though the lower instruments are clearly in 6/8 (see example b).

polyrhythm: A musical texture in which two or more different rhythmic patterns are juxtaposed. Most writers use the term synonymously with polymeter*. In order to identify a polyrhythmic texture the rhythms must hold a specific rhythmic pattern for a long enough span of time so that they may be identified clearly. The following example shows three different rhythms in a polyrhythmic context:

polytonality: The simultaneous use of two or more tonalities. If only two keys are involved, the term bitonality* is appropriate. In polytonal music the individual scales and keys generally retain their identity. The level of dissonance created is in-fluenced by the intervallic relationships of the various tonics involved. For example, if the tonics are a perfect fifth apart, the result may be quite consonant; if they are a tritone* apart, the result will be dissonant. Many composers have used polytonality in their works. Among those who frequently have employed the technique are Igor Stravinsky, Béla Bartók, Darius Milhaud, and William Schuman.

pop art: A type of super-realistic art of the 1960's that took as its focal point the everyday objects of the commonplace world — such as comic strips, automobile fashions, billboards, girlie magazines, and supermarkets — and re-created their manufactured, sterile qualities in painting and sculpture. The pop artist is not so much concerned with finding beauty as he is with commenting on a world of mass-produced goods and vapid impersonalism. The term "pop" is derived from popular, as in popular culture. Outstanding artists in this school include Claes Oldenburg, Jasper Johns, James Rosenquist, Andy Warhol, and George Segal.

pop tune: A popular song designed for wide distribution through the sale of recordings and their inclusion on AM* radio programs.

pot: Abbreviation for potentiometer*.

potentiometer: A variable resistor* used to limit the voltage* in a circuit* by comparing an unknown voltage with a reference voltage. A volume control on an amplifier* is an example of a potentiometer.

preamplifier: A special amplifier* that increases the output* signal* of a low level source to prepare it for processing by a standard amplifier.

precompositional aspect: A property of musical material (e.g., a scale, a mode, a tone* row) that can be classified according to its structural characteristics but may or may not appear in the completed work.

prepared piano: A piano whose playing function and resultant sound have been altered by the introduction, of various rubber, metal, cloth, and wooden objects into its mechanism. This is accomplished in many ways such as weaving felt between the strings, attaching bolts to strings, and placing thumbtacks in hammers. The sounds produced by a prepared piano are resonantly percussive and can vary in pitch definition. Composers John Cage, Henry Cowell, and Edgar Varèse, among others, have written works for this instrument.

prime: The basic form of a twelve-tone* row which may be subjected to inversion*, retrograde*, retrograde-inversion*, or transposition*. See twelve-tone* technique.

prime set: See prime*, set*.

primitive art: 1. The art of so-called primitive peoples in media such as wood, stone, pottery, or metal. The face masks of many African tribes are a good example of primitive art. Many contemporary artists have been influenced by the vitality and variety of the art of primitive peoples, and have incorporated elements of primitive style into their works. Picasso, Derian, Modigliani and Brancusi are notable artists who have been influenced in this manner. Composer Igor Stravinsky was greatly influenced by primitivism as is evidenced in his *Rite of Spring* (1913). 2. Primitive art is also used to denote a style evident in artists such as Henri Rousseau, Edward Hicks and "Grandma" Moses, in which a quasi-naive, technically simple and essentially self-taught manner of technique is utilized.

print-out: Printed data produced by a computer*.

print-through: The inadvertant leakage

of magnetic patterns from one layer of a reel of recording tape to the next layer. See magnetic* tape.

probability theory: A mathematical basis for predicting the likelihood of occurence of a chance event such as when a die is rolled or a coin flipped. The theory of probability can be expressed simply in the following quotient: probability equals the number of occurrences divided by the number of possible occurrences. Various processes in the composition of chance* music are dependent on probability theory.

program: 1. A set of step-by-step instructions that informs a computer* of precisely how to solve a problem automatically. 2. The act of preparing step-by-step instructions for problem solving by a computer.

programming: The process by which problems are analyzed and means of solution prepared in the form of step-by-step instructions that can direct the actions of a computer*.

programming language: A system of symbols used to give instructions to a computer*.

progressive jazz: A term that is used loosely to cover jazz* music of the post-bop* period. Progressive jazz took the intimate, polyphonic, and "cool" sound of bop, mixed in some new instruments (especially flute, flugelhorn, French horn, and accordion), sometimes experimented with meters not commonly found in jazz (e.g., 3/4, 5/4) and generally solidified the often experimental and frenetic sound of bop into a substantial musical form. A good example of progressive jazz would be the music produced by saxophonist Bud Shank and trombonist Bob Brookmeyer on the West Coast in the early 1950's. Some other outstanding names in the progressive jazz movement include Stan Getz, Stan Kenton, Dave Brubeck, Gerry Mulligan, and Shorty Rogers.

projection: Composer Howard Hanson's term for the construction of scales or chords through the utilization of one specific interval, such as a scale built in whole tones or a chord built in perfect fourths.

prolongation: A term from Schenkerian* analysis that denotes interior contrapuntal and harmonic expansion within the larger context of the basic chordal structure. In the process of prolongation, a clear distinction is made between subordinate chords as opposed to the structural pillars of the progression undergoing prolongation. The way in which a particular chordal prolongation is carried out by the composer reveals substantial information regarding his skill in manipulating harmonic and melodic material over large time spans while maintaining compositional direction. In a larger context each subsequent level (background*, middleground*, and foreground*) expands and prolongs the previous level. See Schenkerian* analysis.

Prometheus chord: See mystic* chord.

Prometheus neapolitan scale: The Prometheus* scale with the second degree flatted.

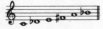

Prometheus scale: A six-note scale based on the mystic* chord of Alexander Scriabin and utilized in his symphonic poem *Prometheus, Poem of Fire* (1910).

proto-tonality: A term coined by composer Lou Harrison as a replacement for atonality*.

psychedelic art: An art style developed during the late 1960's that attempted to create shapes and patterns similar to those perceived by persons under the influence of hallucinatory drugs, particularly LSD. Typical to these works are bright colors in sharply delineated patterns with many curves and swirls in the design.

psychedelic sound: See psychedelic* rock.

psychedelic rock: A general term used to describe rock* music that attempts to create a musical parallel to the feelings induced in people under the effects of drugs, particularly marijuana and LSD. Psychedelic rock is often languid, slow-moving, and sensual. It is meant to serve as a musical background for those listening under the influence of drugs. Light* shows may accompany the music. San Francisco is usually regarded as the home of psychedelic rock, and the Jefferson Airplane is a representative psychedelic rock group.

psychoacoustics: The field of knowledge concerned with how musical stimuli are perceived and recorded by the human listener. The German scientist Hermann Helmholtz is considered to be the first major psychoacoustician. His book *On the Sensations of Tone* (1863) is one of the first works to explore the properties of tone (pitch, quality, etc.) and its effect on the human ear. There has been particular interest in this field during the twentieth century as the sound materials utilized in musical compositions have expanded extensively.

pulse wave: A waveform* produced by sudden voltage* changes from negative to positive to negative. The square* wave is a pulse wave in which the voltage is on for the same amount of time that it is off. Other pulse waves (also called rectangular waves) can be formed by varying the length of time the voltage is on in relation to how long it is off. Pulse waves create the following visual patterns on an oscilloscope*.

punch card: A piece of heavy paper on which data is or can be represented as a pattern of holes. The holes are sensed within a computer* thus introducing information into the system.

punches: Perforations made in motion picture film that result in sudden flashes of light on the projection screen furnishing visual cues for a composer or conductor of film* music.

Putney synthesizer: A small music synthesizer* with optional keyboard. The unit has three independently tunable oscillators* (each with two waveform* outputs), a ring modulator*, a white* noise generator, a reverberation* device, a band-pass* filter, and an envelope* generator. See electronic* music.

pyramidal chord: A chord consisting of a number of intervals whose sizes diminish from bottom to top.

pyramids: A term from the Schillinger* system used to denote orchestral arpeggios sustained as the instruments enter on different pitch levels, each one holding its particular note.

Q

quad: See quadraphonic* sound.

quadraphonic sound: A four-channel* (double stereo*) sound reproduction system that utilizes loudspeakers* in four different locations to increase the spatial feeling first created by stereophonic* sound.

quadrosonic sound: See quadraphonic* sound.

qualitative notation: A term used by Erhard Karoschka in his book *Notation in New Music* (1966) to describe a system of notation developed by Henri Pousseur in which basic time values are organized in approximate durational groups. The performer decides the time limits of the various groups which then remain constant for the entire composition.

quartal harmony: Harmonic formations based on the interval of the fourth. Most often the perfect fourth has been the basic building block of such chords, and composers such as Paul Hindemith and Béla Bartók are well-known for their penchant for quartal harmonies. The example below shows a chord progression based on quartal harmony.

quarten Harmonien: German for quartal* harmony.

quarter-tone: One half of a semi-tone. Using this intervallic division the octave would contain twenty-four quarter-tones. Many composers (e.g., Béla Bartók, Pierre Boulez, Ernest Bloch, Charles Ives, Alois Hába, Karlheinz Stockhausen) have experimented with quarter-tones. Ives wrote *Quarter-tone Chorale for Strings* and *Quarter-tone Pieces for Two Pianos* (1903-1924) among other works in this technique. Hába is the most prolific quarter-tone composer and writer on the subject. In 1923 he established a formal course in quarter-tone technique at the Prague Conservatory. Other composers who have written works using quarter-tones include John Foulds, Miroslov Pong, Ivan Vyschnegradsky, Arthur Lourie, Jörg Mager, and Jan Maklakiewicz. Quarter-tone pianos have been patented by G. A. Behrens-Senegalden (1892), August Foerster (1924), and Hans Barth (1931). Bartók used arrows above and below the standard pitches to indicate quarter-tones, Bloch has used diagonal lines positioned before the standard pitch, and Hába has employed modifications of the traditional sharp and flat signs. No standard quarter-tone notation has ever been agreed upon. See microtonalism*.

quarter-track tape recorder: A tape* recorder principally used for the home reproduction of stereophonic* sound that utilizes tape* heads spanning approximately one-quarter of the width of a quarter-inch magnetic* tape. The heads are arranged so that there is a gap between them equal to their width. In this way tracks one and three can be recorded in one direction and tracks two and four in the other.

quarternion: A group of four parts or elements. In twelve-tone* technique quarternion is used to refer to a tone* row that is constructed so that each successive three-note group has structural significance.

quintal chord: A chord built in intervals of the fifth, usually perfect fifths. Many contemporary composers have employed such chords as a means of avoiding tertian* harmony. In the progression below, chords one, four and five are quintal structures.

R

R: Abbreviation for retrograde*.

Radio Cologne: The first major electronic* music studio was established in Germany at Radio Cologne in 1951 and began operation under the direction of Dr. Herbert Eimert. Other composers associated with

Radio Cologne's studio in its early years were Robert Beyer and Karlheinz Stockhausen.

raga: A scale or melodic mode in Indian music bearing a fixed relationship to the drone (usually performed on the tambura, a stringed instrument producing a fundamental note with a perfect fifth above). A constant tonic is implied throughout the melodic structure of a raga. Most ragas contain a central or chief note ("anska svara") which occurs frequently, with a fixed upper and lower limit implied for a particular raga. Certain melodic characteristics pervade each raga and according to the time of day specific embellishments become more or less desirable. Ragas traditionally were handed down from teacher to pupil without the aid of written notes. Each raga has a specific character or flavor that must be preserved in performance.

ragtime: Essentially cheerful jazz* piano music of the late nineteenth and early twentieth centuries inspired by the military march and the cakewalk*. Ragtime is characterized by a strict duple or quadruple meter with a syncopated melody and a left-hand accompaniment consisting of octaves alternating with chords on the offbeat. Some typical rags include *Frog Legs Rag* (1906), *Maple Leaf Rag* (1899), and *Climax Rag* (1914). Ragtime originated in the Midwest, and both black and white musicians were its composers and performers. Unlike most early jazz music, ragtime was printed on sheet music. Some outstanding figures in the development of ragtime include Scott Joplin, Buddy Bolden, Tom Turpin, Louis Chauvin, and Artie Matthews. Ragtime eventually lost much of its formal stiffness and rigid syncopated quality as it was absorbed into the mainstream of jazz. Igor Stravinsky used this jazz style as a model in his works *Ragtime* for eleven instruments (1918) and *Piano Rag-Music* (1920).

Rahmennotation: German for frame* notation.

ramp wave: See sawtooth* wave.

R and B: Abbreviation for rhythm* and blues.

random access: A computer* system in which the time necessary to store and retrieve information is independent of the storage location.

random generator: An electronic device that produces all frequencies* in the sound* spectrum simultaneously with a random frequency and amplitude* pattern. The resultant sound is known as white* noise. See colored* noise, pink* noise, blue* noise.

random music: See aleatory*, chance* music, indeterminacy*.

random number generator: A computer* program* or a special procedure or device designed to produce random numbers in specific quantities. Random number generators are used by composers to create numerical sequences that can be applied to various parameters* of music such as pitch, rhythm, timbre, and attack.

R and R: See rock* and roll.

rayonism: A short-lived Russian abstract* art movement of the early 1900's in which rays of color were projected into space. Michael Larionov launched this style of painting which was an important step in the development of abstractionism.

RCA synthesizer: The Radio Corporation of America developed the first large-scale synthesizer* and demonstrated it in 1955 under the name of the Olson-Belar Sound Synthesizer. A refined version of this instrument called the Mark II was installed in the newly formed Columbia-Princeton* Electronic Music Center in 1959. The RCA Mark II Synthesizer can generate sounds and control their frequency*, amplitude*, envelope*, and duration. The composer or operator uses two keyboards to punch coded instructions into a roll of paper which controls the operations of the synthesizer causing it to generate and manipulate sound material and record the results on magnetic* tape.

realism: A general term used to designate those concepts and techniques in the arts that contribute to a representation of nature or real life.

realistic sculpture: Sculptures in papier-mâché, plaster, fiber glass, and styrofoam that attempt to be "more real than real." For example, John de Andrea makes plaster casts of the human form and molds a final work in polyester resin or fiber glass which he then paints. Duane Hannon's sculpture entitled *Sunbather* was cast from a real person and molded in plastic. The finished product is amazingly life-like, right down to the suntan lotion, magazine, and tote-bag accompanying the main sculpture. Other artists include Raymond Mason, James Grashow, Nancy Grossman, and Alex Katz. See sharp-focus* realism.

real time: The actual passing of time in relationship to a physical event or process.

real-time performance: The direct and actual control of compositional processes at the time of performance. This is possible in electronic* music and computer* music where many aspects of a work can be created or subjected to modification during a performance. The terms real-time performance and live performance are often used interchangeably.

rebop: See bop*.

record head: The part of a tape recorder that converts fluctuating voltage* into a pattern on magnetic* tape. See tape* recorder, playback* head, erase* head.

rectangular wave: See pulse* wave.

reduction: A procedure common to Schenkerian* analysis in which each successive sketch of the foreground*, middleground*, and background* contains fewer and fewer details until the fundamental skeletal structure is revealed.

reel-to-reel: A tape* recording system in which magnetic* tape is transferred from one spool to another during the recording and playback* processes. See tape* cartridge, cassette*.

referentialism: A philosophic position that declares that the true meaning of artworks involves references to emotions, feelings, and ties to events, people, and images, **outside** of the given work. Art in this context must serve a social and psychological need in order to be effective. It cannot be successful by merely titillating the senses. Referentialism is found in the aesthetic discourses of writers such as Plato, Leo Tolstoy, and Deryck Cooke. See absolute* music.

reflective chord: A vertical* sonority created by adding below a given chord the inverted intervals of that chord. Thus the lower half of a reflective chord is an exact inversion* of the upper half. Chords of this construction are also referred to as mirror chords or symmetrical chords. See involution*.

registration of duration: See duration* series.

Reihe: German for tone* row.

Reihenkomposition: German for tone* row composition. See twelve-tone* music.

relay: A switch that is opened and closed by variations in the current* of an electrical circuit*. Relays are used to control the flow of current in either their own or other circuits and are common to synthesizers* and computers*.

release: See bridge*.

resistance forms: A term from the Schillinger* system used to denote the feeling of suspense or expectation created as a melodic line or harmonic progression moves toward a climax. Schillinger claims that without the proper amount of resistance a dramatic effect will not result at the climactic point.

resistor: A device used in a circuit* to impede the flow of current*.

resultant tone: See combination* tone.

retinal art: See op* art.

retrograde: A backwards statement of a group of notes beginning with the last and proceeding to the first. A motive, a melodic line, a twelve-tone* row, a rhythmic pattern, or a section of a composition may be subjected to retrograde (Paul Hindemith's *Fugue in F* from *Ludus Tonalis* (1943) has a retrograde of the entire first half of the fugue beginning in measure thirty). See example of a retrograde of a twelve-tone row under transformation*.

retrograde-inversion: A backwards statement of the inversion* of a motive, melodic line, or twelve-tone* row. In the following examples the twelve-tone row from Arnold Schoenberg's *Suite* for piano, Op. 25 (1924) is found in its prime* form (example a), its inverted form (example b) and in its retrograde-inverted form (example c):

retrogression: A term sometimes applied to a "weak" harmonic progression, usually one moving away from tonic. Theorist Allen McHose lists some common harmonic retrogressions as follows: dominant to supertonic, dominant to subdominant, and dominant to mediant. It should be pointed out that much rock* music relies on retrogressions as a basic stylistic feature, often in extended stepwise harmonic sequences such as I-bVII-bVI-V-IV-I.

reverberation unit: An electronic device that continuously repeats in decreasing amplitude* an original signal* creating the illusion of closely-spaced echoes*.

rhythm and blues: A variety of urban folk-blues marked by strong, repetitious rhythms, simple melodic structure, and basic harmonic progressions gravitating around I, IV, and V. Rhythm and blues is a stylistic descendant of what was called "rare" music or "sepia" blues prior to World War II. There is a close relationship between rhythm and blues and early rock* and roll. Up to the middle 1950's rhythm and blues was almost entirely the domain of black musicians such as Little Richard, Chubby Checker, Fats Domino and B.B. King. A typical rhythm and blues combo features a tenor saxophonist who performs in a "honking" or screeching style, sometimes lying on his back while performing. See blues*.

rhythmic displacement: The repetition of a harmonic or melodic segment with a different relationship to the meter in which it is found.

rhythmic invariance: Continuous rhythmic motion. See Fortspinnung*.

rhythmicon: An electronic* musical instrument designed by composer Henry Cowell and built by Leon Theremin (see theremin*) that was capable of performing rhythmic combinations of almost unlimited complexity. In 1931 Cowell wrote *Rhythmicana,* a concerto for rhythmicon and orchestra.

RI: Abbreviation for retrograde-inversion*.

ribbon controller: A linear* controller through which pitch can be continuously varied by sliding a finger along a band of metal.

riff: A short figure or phrase in jazz* that is usually repeated while the harmony changes below it. Sometimes the riff will move from section to section (e.g., brass to saxes) in a big* band; or in smaller ensemble improvisation* riffs might be traded back and forth between the soloists.

F7   Bb7   F7   D7

RILM: An acronym for "Repertoire International de la Litterature Musicale" (which can be translated as International Repertory of Music Literature), a long-range plan that uses the computer* to gain bibliographic control of scholarly literature concerning music. RILM is jointly sponsored by the International Musicological Society and the International Association of Music Libraries.

rimshot: A percussion sound made when the rim and head of a snare drum are struck at the same time. This technique is common in jazz*.

ringing: A carry-over effect sometimes generated by electrical components as they continue to respond to signals* that have ceased.

ring modulator: An electronic* device which accepts two channels* of input*, derives the sum and difference in frequency* of these two channels, subtracts the original two difference frequencies to a single frequencies, and feeds the sum and output*. Ring modulators are used as sound modifiers in electronic* music composition.

rip: A rapid glissando moving into a specific tone which is articulated sharply upon arrival. This effect is commonly performed by jazz* brass and woodwind players. The rip is indicated by either of the two methods listed below.

rise time: The time between the beginning of a sound and the point at which it reaches maximum amplitude*. (Also referred to as the attack.) See envelope*.

RIT: An abbreviation used to indicate a transposed retrograde-inversion* of a twelve-tone* row.

RMS power: The sustained power capacity of an amplifier* at a specific distortion* level.

rock: See rock* and roll.

rock and roll: A general term (with sexual implications, as rockin' and rollin' originally meant fornicating) used to cover many styles and types of music since the early 1950's. Early rock groups such as Bill Haley and the Comets (see hard* rock), The Everly Brothers, and individuals such as Elvis Presley, Little Richard, and Fats Domino started the rock craze which filled a need that popular music and jazz* were unable to satisfy. As time passed rock groups became more sophisticated and musically inventive. Groups such as the Beatles, the Byrds, the Jefferson Airplane, and the Mothers of Invention mixed folk, jazz, and country music into an over-all rock sound. The blues* also came into renewed focus under the aegis of groups such as the Blues Project and the Animals. The most influential rock group during the 1960's was the Beatles. Early rock was heavily dependent on basic triadic

chord progressions like I-VI-II-V-I and I-IV-V-I. However, rock music of the late 1960's contains more complicated harmonic relationships, and a greater use of modal progressions sometimes reminiscent of Renaissance style. Many rock groups of the late 1960's and early 1970's fused jazz elements into the basic rock sound. A group such as Blood, Sweat, and Tears not only shows a great jazz influence, but also has incorporated elements of electronic* music, musique* concrète, bossa nova*, and country music into a truly eclectic idiom.

root clouding: The phenomenon that occurs when ninth*, eleventh*, and thirteenth* chords include so many altered notes that the traditional function of the chord root is not apparent to the ear.

rootless harmony: Harmonic structures that lack a clear root function due to their equidistant intervallic construction. Chords built in perfect fourths, major seconds, minor thirds (e.g., diminished chords), and major thirds (e.g., augmented chords) fall into this category.

rotary motion: A term from the Schillinger* system used to denote the movement of a melody circulating above an axis* which produces a wave-like curve when graphed. This movement may be based on spirals, circular forms of various types, or sine forms.

rotation: The systematic and successive rearrangement of the pitches of a given tone* row. This can be accomplished by applying a single factor (e.g., beginning the row on its second note), a number of factors (e.g., beginning the row on its second note and progressing with every other note), or a serially devised plan.

routine: A sequence of instructions designed to cause a computer* to perform a specific task.

rovescio: An Italian term synonymous with retrograde*. It is also used on occasion to refer to melodic inversion*.

row: See tone* row.

RT: An abbreviation used to indicate a transposed retrograde* of a twelve-tone* row.

rumble: Undesirable low frequency* noise produced through an amplifier* due to minute vibrations in the turntable*.

S

S: Abbreviation for set*.

samba: A Brazilian dance in slow tempo based on the following rhythmic pattern:

sawtooth wave: A waveform* containing the fundamental* frequency* and all of its overtones* with the amplitude* of each overtone inversely proportional to its position in the harmonic* series. In this waveform the voltage* slowly ascends to positive and then instantly descends to negative producing the following visual pattern on an oscilloscope*:

scaling: The perceptual distance between certain basic stimuli (e.g., sounds and colors) that can be readily measured by a computer* analysis of data.

scat singing: Jazz* singing using nonsense syllables. Louis Armstrong and Cab Calloway were among the earliest pioneers in scat singing, and in the early bop* period Dizzy Gillespie became known for his facility in this style. Sometimes the singer imitates the sound of an instrument in addition to singing nonsense syllables. A typical bop scat line would use syllables such as "oo-bop-she-bam" or "eel-ya-dah". Certain jazz singers such as Mel Torme and Ella Fitzgerald have developed scat styles of great complexity.

Schenkerian analysis: A system of musical analysis developed by the Austrian theorist Heinrich Schenker (1868-1935), and carried forth by such American writers as Felix Salzer and Allen Forte. The Schenker system has had a great influence on twentieth century composers and theorists interested in the architectonic* aspects of musical composition. Forte states that through Schenker's concept of structural* levels a fundamental principle is set forth that opens the way for the understanding of new meanings and relationships in music. Schenker's system attempts to disclose the basic organic form that music achieves, through the utilization and elaboration of basic tone structures, chord progressions, and musical lines. Schenker as a theorist, like Paul Hindemith, is dependent upon natural acoustical phenomena (e.g., the overtone series). His concept of structural levels in many ways revolutionized analytic thinking, especially in the notion that the middleground* is where a composer's genius may be demonstrated. Theorist Edward Cone has pointed out that part of the greatest of Schenker stems from the fact that his system reveals how a piece of music should be **heard**, in that it shows how basic patterns and cells unfold into a complete composition. Critics of Schenker have pointed out that there are numerous problems connected with his system, such as: 1. Too much concern with scale steps and step progression; 2. Why not five, eight, or ten structural levels as the situation necessitates rather than three? 3. Too much concern with descending lines to the exclusion of all others; 4. Not enough concern for the significance of rhythm. Whatever validity there may be to these criticisms it is clear that Schenker has been a major force in theoretical thinking. See architectonic* levels, background*, composing-out*, foreground*, Grundbrechung*, middleground*, prolongation*, Urlinie*, Ursatz*.

Schichten: German for structural* levels.

Schillinger system: A system of composition developed by Joseph Schillinger during the 1930's that applies principles of mathematical logic to the various materials of music such as rhythm, harmony, melody, counterpoint, orchestration, and composition. Schillinger's system was adopted by certain schools (e.g., the Julliard School of Music and the Music Department at Columbia University) as well as by some notable musicians (e.g., George Gershwin, Glenn Miller, Alvino Rey, Will Bradley, Paul Lavalle, and Benny Goodman). Schillinger attempted to discover the general underlying forces and principles that shape musical phenomena and to classify the various resources of tonal music. To Schillinger, great art music reproduced basic laws or processes found in the universe and could be explicated through mathematical models. Schillinger favored scientific planning in addition to the need for creative intuition when composing music. In this regard he discriminated between the different perceptual aspects of time as it relates to the psychology and physiology of listening. Schillinger went as far as to suggest how composers such as Bach and Beethoven could have "improved" their compositions if they had been able to employ certain of his compositional and mathematical principles. See axis* relations, circular* permutation, coupling*, original* primitive, pre-set*, pyramids*, resistance* forms, rotary* motion, series* of acceleration, stylized* primitive scale, temporal* saturation.

scordatura: A retuning of a string instrument in order to produce notes not usually available on the strings tuned in a standard arrangement. In Stravinsky's *Rite of Spring* (1913), for example, the violoncelli at rehearsal number 90 retune their C strings to B natural in order to produce an F♯ harmonic on that string at 91.

secondary set: A term used by composer and theorist Milton Babbitt to describe a twelve-tone* row created when the first hexachord* of one set-form* of an original* row is followed by the second hexachord of a different set-form (or vice versa). The two set-forms must possess the property of combinatoriality* so that there is no duplication of pitches within the secondary set. Example (a) below indicates the original* form of the tone row used in Babbitt's *Three Compositions for Piano No. 1* (1947). Example (b) indicates a secondary set formed by the second hexachord of the original followed by the first hexachord of the inversion* of the row transposed up a perfect fifth.

second order set: A term originated by composer and theorist Milton Babbitt to designate a source* set that creates combinatorial relationships at two different levels of transposition*. See combinatoriality*.

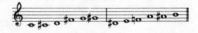

secundal chord: Any chord constructed primarily in intervals of major or minor seconds.

segmentation: The division of a twelve-tone* row into two hexachords*, three segments of four tones, or four segments of three tones. Segmentation allows for more flexible motivic treatment and facilitates the use of contrapuntal devices in twelve-tone* technique. See derivation* technique, partition*.

self-thread reels: A tape* recorder take-up reel with adhesive or some other special device on the hub that holds the tape in place.

sel-sync: An electronic circuit* that is used in tape* recording to synchronize the recording of a new track* with previously recorded material on other tracks. In the normal operation of a tape* recorder, there is a time lag between recording and monitoring because the heads* that control these two functions are separated. A sel-sync system uses the record* head to both record and monitor, thus doing away with any time lag. This device is most helpful in electronic* music composition where layer upon layer of sound must be synchronized in the recording process.

semi-acoustical guitar: A type of hybrid guitar that is a cross between the acoustical* guitar and the electric* guitar. A hollow resonating body is coupled with an electric apparatus. The semi-acoustical guitar may be played without amplification, although it is generally not loud enough to be used in live performance situations.

semi-combinatorial set: A twelve-tone* row constructed in such a way that the first six notes (hexachord*) of

one of its transposed transformations*, excluding retrograde*, do not duplicate any of the first six notes of the original* row. See combinatoriality*, all-combinatorial* set.

semitonal scale: Another term for chromatic scale.

semitonic scale: Another term for chromatic scale.

sequencer: See sequential* controller.

sequential controller: An electronic device used in a synthesizer* to program discrete voltage* changes which can be used to control the amplitude* of a voltage-controlled* amplifier, the frequency* of a voltage-controlled oscillator, and to supply rhythmic patterns through triggers* to envelope* generators. Each discrete voltage is adjustable through manual* controls.

sequential programmer: See sequential* controller.

serialism: See serial* music.

serialized duration: See duration* series.

serialized harmony: Harmonic structures derived from a tone* row, particularly a twelve-tone* row. For example, the row in example (a) might yield the chords found in example (b).

serialized melody: A melody derived from a tone* row, particularly a twelve-tone* row. For example, the tone row found in example (a) below might lend itself to the melodic design in example (b).

serialized rhythm: See duration* series.

serial music: A generic term applied to music employing serial or twelve-tone* techniques. Generally, serial music is an attempt to forge a new musical language exclusive of the tenets of tonality and many of the general stylistic by-products of tonal music such as traditional melodic lines, chord structures based on tertian* or quartal* harmonic schemes, and a strong metric-rhythmic pulse interaction. Originally serial techniques were concerned with pitch alone, but later developments included the serialization of other parameters* of music, resulting in total* control. Some writers prefer the use of the term serial for music in which not just the twelve-tones are preordered, but also dynamics, rhythmic values, densities, and registers. It is possible, of course, to preorder a row containing more or fewer than twelve-tones. See duration* series.

serial procedures: See twelve-tone* music and serial* music.

SERIES: A specialized computer* program* devised by G.M. Koenig of the University of Bonn which functions as a subroutine* for generating tone* rows of various lengths. See ALEA*.

series: 1. A term synonymous with set* and tone* row in twelve-tone* music that denotes a particular ordering of the twelve pitches within an octave. 2. A specific succession of pitches or other elements of music (e.g., durations, modes of attack, dynamic levels).

series of acceleration: A term from the Schillinger* system used to denote any numerical series in which there is an increasing or decreasing differential between successive terms. Examples of such patterns would include a natural series such as 1, 2, 3, 4, 5, etc.; prime number series such as 1, 3, 5, 7, etc.; or a power series such as 3, 9, 27, 81, 243, etc. Such series are crucial to an understanding of Schillinger's theory of rhythm which is dependent upon principles of regularity and coordination as patterns evolve in a universal configuration.

series I: Paul Hindemith's term (from his book *The Craft of Musical Composition* [1941]), for a succession of the twelve chromatic tones derived through various relationships within the harmonic* series from a progenitor tone, resulting in a "family relationship" inclusive of all these tones. The tones are ranked in order of importance and their significance lies in the fact that they become the basis for harmonic and tonal connections and relationships in Hindemith's system. The eleven derived tones are ranked from strongest to weakest in such a way as to form the following eleven intervals with the progenitor tone: perfect fifth, perfect fourth, major sixth, major third, minor third, minor sixth, major second, minor seventh, minor second, major seventh, and tritone*.

set: A specific group or succession of notes used as a point of departure for compositional processes. Composer and theorist Milton Babbitt first introduced the term in 1946 in his article "The Function of Set Structure in the Twelve-tone System". At this time it applied primarily to a specific succession of the twelve notes of the chromatic scale and was synonymous with twelve-tone* row and series*. The term set now has a broader and more general implication as well, including tone* rows of fewer or more than twelve tones and successions of notes that do not stem from twelve-tone* technique.

set-complex: The forty-eight different forms of a given twelve-tone* row (set*) created by transposing each of its transformations* (prime*, inversion*, retrograde*, retrograde-inversion*) to all twelve pitch levels of the chromatic scale. See set* theory, twelve-tone* technique, transposition*.

set-form: Any one of the forty-eight different forms of a twelve-tone* row created by transposing each of the row's four transformations* (prime*, inversion*, retrograde*, retrograde-inversion*) to all twelve pitch levels of the chromatic scale. See set-complex*.

set number: See order* number, order-number* pitch-number couple.

set table: See set-complex*.

set theory: The detailed study and analysis of pitch and rhythmic relationships that generally stem from twelve-tone* techniques. Composers and theorists Milton Babbitt, George Perle and George Rochberg have been particularly active writers on this subject. See set*, combinatoriality*, derivation* technique, aggregate*, source* set, trope*, secondary* set.

seventeenth chord: A tertian* sonority with a basic structure consisting of nine different notes. It can be viewed as a combination of three triads.

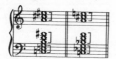

shake: A jazz effect somewhat like a wide trill. Shakes are usually employed by brass players, or, in big* bands, by the entire brass section on occasion. The instrument is rocked or shaken to produce the effect, although some players are adept at lip shakes as well. The shake is indicated in the following manner.

sharp-focus realism: An art movement of the early 1970's growing out of the pop* art movement that was characterized by paintings that appear to be as realistic as photographs. Most of the artists working in this style use photographs as the "model" for a given canvas, and show a penchant for subject matter such as automobiles, trucks, kitchenware, street scenes, or the human figure. *Rustler Charger* by Richard McLean is a good example of sharp-focus realism. A man on a horse is shown receiving a prize from a woman at a horse show. From the tiniest pebble on the ground to the large sign in the background the effect is one of super-photographic realism. Other artists in this movement include Alfred Leslie, William Bailey, Philip Pearlstein, Chuck Close and Richard Estes.

shifting meter: See multimeter*.

SHMRG: A system of stylistic analysis set forth by musicologist Jan LaRue that encompasses the following elements or categories: S) Sound (e.g., range, tessitura, dynamics, timbre); H) Harmony (e.g., tonality, chord vocabulary, dissonance, progressions, sequences); M) Melody (e.g., chromatic, diatonic, pattern, mode, articulation); R) Rhythm (e.g., meter, tempo, pulse, motive, stress); G) Growth (e.g., balance and relationship between movements, overlap, elision, development).

sideman: A musician in a jazz* ensemble other than the leader.

signal: A series of electrical impulses* representing audio* or video* information.

signal-to-noise ratio: The ratio of desired signal* voltage* to random noise voltage as expressed in decibels*. The more background noise that can be eliminated the better the signal-to-noise ratio will be, and the higher the decibel level will be.

signal transfer: See print-through*.

simultaneity: A collection of notes sounded at the same time. This term is often used by serial* composers to indicate situations in which adjacent notes of a twelve-tone* row are sounded together.

simultaneous meters: See polymeter*.

sine wave: A waveform* containing the fundamental* frequency* with no overtones*. This produces a so-called "pure" tone. In this waveform the voltage* is varied, slowly increasing and decreasing from negative to positive to negative, producing the following visual pattern on an oscilloscope*:

sine wave generator: An oscillator* that produces only sine* waves.

sinusoidal wave: The full name for sine* wave.

sinus tone: See sine* wave.

Six, Les: A group of French composers consisting of Darius Milhaud, Louis Durey, Francis Poulenc, Germaine Tailleferre, Georges Auric and Arthur Honegger who banded together around 1917-1921 to further the artistic and aesthetic precepts of the writer Jean Cocteau. Basically the group was opposed to the impressionistic* style and hoped to forge a return to clarity and directness in music. They had a great interest in the popular music of their day such as ragtime*, jazz*, dance hall, and cabaret music.

six-tone scale: See hexatonic* scale.

sizzle cymbal: A cymbal common to jazz* and rock* music that is made in various sizes and usually is mounted on a tall metal stand. Metal rivets are loosely fitted around the rim of the cymbal, and when the cymbal is struck (usually with a snare drum stick) the rivets vibrate, causing a sizzling sound.

skiffle: Jazz* as performed on rudimentary instruments such as combs, jugs, washboard, kazoos, and bottles.

skiffle band: A band using skiffle* instruments.

slap pizzicato: A jazz* effect whereby the bass viol player plucks the string with such force that it strikes the neck of the bass creating a slapping sound.

slap tongue: A jazz* effect created when the performer strikes his tongue against the mouthpiece. The effect is simply called "slap" when a bass player plucks the string vigorously so that it strikes the neck of the bass.

smear: A jazz* effect in which a tone is approached from below and slid into in the form of a short glissando. Common to the blues* and pieces in slower tempi, the smear places more emphasis on the move into the pitch than the arrival on the pitch. A smear is indicated by a wavy line over the note.

smoothing filter: An electronic filter* that removes or reduces unwanted high-frequency components of a sound* wave.

snap pizzicato: A string technique invented by Béla Bartók. The snap pizzicato is produced when the performer plucks the string with violent force, rebounding it off the fingerboard. The notation for snap pizzicato consists of a circle with a line emanating from the center, as in the following example:

sneak start: A technique used in film* music in which music is introduced as unobstrusively as possible, frequently under the cover of a sound effect.

SNOBOL: A computer* programming* language developed at the Bell* Laboratories in 1962 and used to process data that is primarily sequential in character. SNOBOL is very useful in operations that involve the scanning of large amounts of information. Theorist Allen Forte has used it in computer studies of the structure of atonal* music.

social realism: A movement in the visual arts of the 1920's and 1930's that favored a supposedly realistic portrayal of the inequities and failures of the capitalist system. It reached its pinnacle during the Depression and was commonly identified with socialist and communist political ideologies. Artists connected with the movement include Ben Shahn, George Bellows, Renato Guttoso, and John Sloan.

sock chorus: The final chorus as played by a large jazz* band that has special drive and fervor. It is typically performed by the entire ensemble. See out* chorus.

soft rock: Rock* music emanating from California that has a lighter, more airy and looser feeling than other rock styles. The music of the Beach Boys, the Mamas and the Papas, and the Fifth Dimension is often identified with this style.

software: Programs*, routines*, manuals, and other documents used in computer* operations.

solid-body guitar: A guitar whose body is formed by a solid material such as plastic which does not resonate when the instrument is played. See electric* guitar.

solid-state: A term referring to the use of semiconductors in circuitry. A semiconductor is an electronic device such as a transistor* or a diode that uses solid material instead of a vacuum to conduct an electrical charge. Typical solid-state materials are silicon and germanium. Solid-state components are more efficient than vacuum devices; they create less heat in operation and their smaller size allows for compactness. Hence, they are ideal for small radios, hearing aids, phonograph and tape* playback* systems, and music synthesizers*.

solovox: A monophonic* electronic* musical instrument manufactured by the Hammond Instrument Company. It is ordinarily attached to and used with a piano. The performer's right hand plays the melody on the solovox while the left hand furnishes an accompaniment on the piano. Loudness is controlled by a knee lever and five tone-control switches are used to vary the timbre*.

sone: A subjective measuring unit for the loudness of a sound which in the judgment of a given listener is equal to the loudness of a 1000 Hz* reference sound at 40 decibels*.

sone scale: See sone*.

sonic imperialism: A term coined by composer R. Murray Schafer that denotes the need many persons feel to constantly shatter quiet with some type of music or noise.

sonido trece: A term used by the Mexican composer Julián Carrillo to describe his compositions using intervals smaller than half or whole tones. Carrillo was one of the first composers to use a microtonal* system and he built his own instruments such as the octavina with forty-eight tones per octave and the arpa citera with ninety-six tones to the octave. Carrillo believed fervently in his musical systems and felt that the future of music would rest upon microtonal manipulations. See microtonalism*.

sonority: See vertical* sonority.

son scale: See sone*.

soul: A vague term used to designate the music created by black artists such as Diana Ross, Ray Charles, James Brown, Gladys Knight and the Pips, Aretha Franklin, and Wilson Pickett. Soul became nationally popular during the 1960's and its essence is in no small way connected to the broader concept of black identity since it is black music performed by black artists, heard primarily on black radio stations and publicized by black magazines and newspapers. Perhaps the most important aspect of soul is its honesty and earthy, unrefined musical quality. See rhythm* and blues, motown*.

sound mass: A combination of pitched and/or pitchless sounds in which individual tones are unimportant, obscure, and often imperceptible.

sound-on-sound: A tape* recording process in which two channels* of information are combined by recording one signal* on a track* containing another previously recorded signal.

soundscape: A term coined by composer R. Murray Schafer that denotes the total environmental world of sound as perceived by the human ear. Automobile sounds, jackhammers, jet airplanes, conversational sounds, etc., all would be component parts of the soundscape. See musique concrète.

sound spectrum: All audible frequencies* that are components of a given complex sound*.

sound synthesis: The creation of sounds through electronic means. See synthesizer*.

sound track: The portion of a 35MM film used for storing audio information. See magnetic* track, optical* track.

sound waves: See waveforms*.

source set: A term originated by composer and theorist Milton Babbitt that refers to a basic, scalar, precompositional* twelve-tone* row whose hexachords* possess the property of combinatoriality*. A source set can

generate a number of different tone rows that can be associated vertically (see aggregate*) without repetition of notes in close proximity.

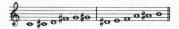

space-time concept: The tendency in contemporary art and music to view both time and space in a massive, overall context, rather than in the older sense of a linear continuum. Hence, in music, events* may be related from back to front (chronologically speaking) or from top to bottom instead of always from front to back, or first to last.

spans of structure: A term coined by theorist Allen Forte that denotes relationships between melodic and harmonic structures over time spans of various lengths. For example, "large span" would refer to the tonal compass of a composition, whereas "small span" would refer to smaller tonal configurations within a given work. Forte indicates that there is a similarity between his spans of structure and Schenker's foreground*, middleground*, and background*, except that the latter do not give as much weight to the time dimension in analysis.

spatial modulation: Varying the location of a sound image within an acoustical environment created by two or more loudspeakers*. See panning*.

speaker: See loudspeaker*.

speaker efficiency: The relative ability of a speaker system to convert electrical energy into sound at specific volume levels.

speech melody: See Sprechstimme*.

sphärophon: An electronic* musical instrument utilizing a keyboard* controller that was invented by Jörg Mager in Berlin and first demonstrated at the Donaueschingen Chambermusic Festival in 1926. The sphärophon was a melodic instrument that was capable of producing microtones*. Timbre as well as pitch could be controlled. In 1931 Mager used this instrument to produce the bell-tones of Wagner's *Parsifal* at Bayreuth.

spherophone: See sphärophon.

Spiegelbild: See retrograde*.

Spielmusik: A German term for music that is written to be played or sung in the home by the amateur musician.

spill: A jazz* effect in which the player reaches a given pitch and loosely "spills" out a gliss rather freely in the manner of a drop-off from the central pitch.

spiral mesh reverberation unit: An electronic device developed by the Electronic Music Studio at the University of Toronto which serves both as a reverberation* unit and as a source for concrete sounds. The main component is a tightly-stretched steel mesh that may be touched or scraped with various materials in order to produce sounds. The reverberation time is about eleven seconds for very low tones.

spiritual: A type of song that sprang from the slave culture in the United States. The public at large was exposed to spirituals after the Civil War. Spirituals were of many types, including work songs, religious songs, and blues* songs. Marshall Stearns has pointed out that the type of spiritual most people are familiar with is actually a rare type, slow-moving and rather lugubrious, as opposed to the more common type of spiritual characterized by great enthusiasm and jubilation. Some popular spirituals are *Swing Low, Sweet Chariot* and *Take This Hammer.* See blues*.

splicer: A device used to measure, cut, and connect pieces of magnetic* tape or film.

splicing tape: A special gummed tape used to connect pieces of magnetic* tape or film.

split channel recording: A technique used in film* music in which a vocalist and an accompanying orchestra are recorded simultaneously but on separate tracks*. In this way the vocal track can be edited without effecting the orchestral track.

spoils of war: A percussion instrument invented by composer Harry Partch which has a single resonator five feet tall and is played by various kinds of mallets. The instrument uses two cloud-chamber* bowls and brass artillery casings to produce basically microtonal* sounds. A device called a whang gun is a part of the spoils of war, producing a "whang" sound by means of a piece of spring steel controlled by a pedal device.

spotting: The determination by a composer of film* music as to precisely where music should begin and end in relation to picture action.

Sprechgesang: A literal translation from the German would be "speech song." This term is often used interchangeably with Sprechstimme*. However, a distinction is sometimes drawn between the two with Sprechgesang referring to the performance technique and Sprechstimme to the actual voice part.

Sprechstimme: A literal translation from the German would be "speech part", a voice part in music which only approximates pitch content but follows the rhythmic values strictly. Sprechstimme is usually indicated by an approximate pitch with an X through the stem of the note. Some composers choose to use the X by itself with a beam or flag attached, while others prefer a round 0 with a stem or flag. Perhaps the best-known work employing Sprechstimme is Arnold Schoenberg's *Pierrot Lunaire* (1912). Other composers such as Alban Berg (*Wozzeck* [1925] and *Lulu* [1937]), Luciano Berio (*Circles* [1960]), and Vladimir Vogel (*Jonah*) have also employed Sprechstimme.

square wave: A waveform* containing the fundamental* frequency* and all odd-numbered overtones* (1, 3, 5, 7, etc.) with the amplitude* of each overtone inversely proportional to its position in the harmonic* series (1, 1/3, 1/5, 1/7, etc.). In this waveform the voltage* is suddenly positive and then suddenly negative producing the following visual pattern on an oscilloscope*. (See pulse* wave).

squeezing: The rushing or slowing down of a segment of film* music in order to make it fit a given picture sequence.

standard tune: A popular song that has endured and hence constitutes an important segment of the music repertoire. When a jazz* musician speaks of a "standard" he is referring to a well-known song such as *Stella by Starlight* (1946) or *How High the Moon* (1940) which lends itself to a variety of treatments in improvisation*. A jazz piece like *Night in Tunisia* (1944) by Dizzy Gillespie can also be thought of as a standard, although it springs from jazz more than from the popular music idiom.

steady-state: That part of a sound, characterized by a constant amplitude* that begins after the attack phase (or rise* time) and ends prior to the decay* phase. See envelope*.

stereo: See stereophonic* sound.

stereophonic sound: Sound reproduction via two or more channels, recreating the effect of the original performance in terms of highs, lows, and spatial orientation.

step progression: Paul Hindemith's term from his book *The Craft of Musical Composition* (1941) for the "line" that connects one melodic high point to the next, or the low point of a melody to the next low point. The "guideposts" found in these lines regulate the horizontal and vertical framework of the composition, and may be considered to be the pivotal notes of a melody. The notes of the step progression form a progression in seconds and in this respect are very similar to the Urlinie* in Schenkerian* analysis. A complicated melodic line may contain several step progressions operating simultaneously.

stepwise progression: Theorist Joseph Yasser's term equivalent to step* progression.

stirrer: A sound panning* device developed by composer Lowell Cross that employs four potentiometers* and is manipulated by turning a crank. The stirrer makes it possible to synchronize the spatial* modulation of four different signals*.

stochastic: 1. A term that pertains to trial-and-error as opposed to step-by-step computer* procedures. 2. Any process that is random or involved with continuous variables.

stochastic music: Music based on statistical calculations that are derived from probability* distribution. *Achorripsis* (1956-7) by Iannis Xenakis is a stochastic work as are many other of his computer* compositions including *ST/48-1, 240162* (1962) and *Atrees* (1962). See stochastic*.

stock arrangement: An arrangement for a dance or jazz* band published in mass quantities. A distinction is usually made between a stock arrangement (available on the open market) and special arrangements (specials) which are usually written for a particular ensemble and are not widely disseminated.

stomp: A "hot" jazz* or blues* tune with a heavy beat. A distinction is sometimes made between the dynamic quality of a stomp tune which induces dancing and movement, and the more reserved or contemplative quality of other jazz tunes.

stop-time: A type of accompanimental situation in which the ensemble plays only the first beat or chord in successive measures while a dancer (e.g., tap dancer) carries on a special pyrotechnical display of technique.

storage: An electronic device that accepts data and stores it until the data is needed and retrieved. See computer*, disk* storage, buffer*.

strategic music: Music that employs game* theory as a procedure in the compositional process.

streamer: A line made by scratching the surface of motion picture film that moves from left to right across the projection screen furnishing a visual cue for a composer or comductor of film* music.

streams: See planing*.

stride piano: A kind of jazz* piano style made famous by men such as Fats Waller, Teddy Wilson, Albert Ammons and Willie (the Lion) Smith, in which a chord on the weak beats and a single note or octave on the strong beats occur in a left hand accompaniment figure. This style of playing became popular during the 1920's and the name was coined because of the striding effect created by the left hand.

stroboconn: A special kind of stroboscope* used to tune musical instruments. The stroboconn, designed and manufactured by C.G. Conn, Ltd., consists of a neon lamp that flashes at the same frequency* as a pitch being applied to it through a microphone*. A set of twelve disks revolving at different speeds corresponding to the equal tempered scale are illuminated by the flashing lamp. If the frequency of the pitch is the same as the speed of a disk, a pattern on the disk appears to remain stationary. If the pitch is flat the pattern appears to move to the left, and if sharp, to the right.

stroboscope: An electronic device used to determine visually the frequency* of a sound. See stroboconn*.

structural levels: See Schenkerian* analysis, foreground*, middleground*, and background*.

Stufen: German for "steps", theorist Heinrich Schenker's term for the major bass components or controlling bass motion in a background* sketch. These bass components have more structural significance than the melodic patterns of the bass at the foreground* or middleground* levels. See Schenkerian* analysis.

stylized primitive scale: A term from the Schillinger* system used to denote an original* primitive scale adapted to diatonic usage in Western music.

sub-infra atonal scale: Theorist Joseph Yasser's term for a scale with five equidistant and independent tones to the octave. He relates this scale to the Salendro scale of Javanese music which originates from the division of the octave into five equal intervals.

sub-infra diatonic scale: Theorist Joseph Yasser's term for a diatonic scale of the "lowest order". This scale contains two regular and three auxiliary degrees, giving it a 2+3 formula. The two diatonic or regular notes are a perfect fourth and perfect fifth apart (e.g., C-F or F-C), and the three auxiliary notes coincide with the tones D, G, and A of the infra-diatonic* scale. Yasser stresses the fact that the predominating number of auxiliary degrees in this primitive scale is its outstanding feature.

subroutine: A computer* routine* that functions as part of another routine.

subset: A segment of a tone* row that has compositional significance as an independent unit. For example, in Anton Webern's *Concerto for Nine Instruments,* Op. 24 (1935), the tone row that serves as the point of departure is derived from a three-note subset. See example under derivation* technique. See set*.

super-dominant: A dominant seventh chord with added and altered tones (e.g., major thirteenth, flatted ninth, and augmented eleventh). Super-dominant chords function as dominant sonorities with increased complexity and drive due to the additions above the basic seventh chord structure.

superimposition: 1. The technique of building complex vertical* sonorities by placing one chord structure over another. See polychord*. 2. The technique of placing a sheet of transparent paper over music manuscript paper so that the imperfections on the transparent paper can be traced as notes onto the paper below. See paper* flyspeck.

super Locrian scale: A synthetic* scale derived from the ancient church mode of the same name (Locrian) that has the following interval structure:

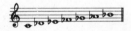

supra-diatonic scale: Theorist Joseph Yasser's term for a scale comprised of twelve regular and seven auxiliary* degrees (giving it a "formula" of 12+7); the former group somewhat equivalent to the present chromatic scale and the latter group much like the present diatonic scale. The supra-diatonic scale of nineteen tones may be achieved by dividing the octave into nineteen equal parts, or by generating nineteen superimposed "natural" fifths, as shown in the following example.

7 auxiliary degrees

F-C-G-D-A-E-B-F♯- C♯- G♯-D♯-A♯- E♯-B♯- F✕- C✕-G✕-D✕-A✕

12 regular degrees

surrealism: A movement in literature and art influenced by Dada* and Freudian concepts of the subconscious, particularly the importance of dreams in the expression of bizarre thoughts and curious juxtapositions. The poet André Breton issued his *First Manifesto of Surrealism* in 1924, which stated the basic premises of the movement. Surrealism as conceived by Breton was virtually a way of life, not just a philosophic/artistic movement. Typical surrealistic canvases present a disquieting mood of dream-like silence, filled with strange visions of objects such as melting watches being devoured by insects. Important artists include Salvador Dali, Yves Tanguy, Max Ernst, James Ensor and Giorgio de Chirico.

surrogate kithara: An instrument invented and built by composer Harry Partch in 1953 that contains several redwood resonators, each one activated by eight strings. The instrument takes roughly the form of a triangle 40 by 40 by 36 inches with an attached seat for the player. It is played with picks, mallets, fingers, or felted sticks. Mandolin tuning heads are used to control pitch settings.

suspended tonality: The phenomenon that occurs when a section of a tonal work temporarily loses its feeling of key center in favor of ambiguous harmonic relationships and of treating tones largely without regard to their place in any major or minor scale.

sweetener: A term used in film* music to refer to a musical effect that is added to the sound* track sometime after the original recording.

swing: 1. A manner of feeling indigenous to jazz* in which rhythms are stretched and staggered to create a particular inflection. It is almost impossible to notate the precise rhythm of a jazz line, but a figure such as the one found in example (a) below would probably be altered by the player to create an effect somewhere **between** examples (b) and (c).

Gunther Schuller has pointed out that the main components of a swing feeling are a forward-propelling directionality to a line, a steady and regular pulse background, an equilibrium between the horizontal and vertical relationship of sounds, an emphasis on the weak beats (backbeats), and the type of rhythmic inflection found in the examples above. 2. Swing also designates the period of large dance bands of the late 1930's and early 1940's. Bands such as those of Benny Goodman, Artie Shaw, Harry James, Fletcher Henderson, and Tommy Dorsey stressed ensemble playing of great precision in which the band often backed a soloist or a singer. Big bands were popular on college campuses, in nightclubs, and in large movie theaters such as the Paramount in New York. See jazz*, big* band.

switch: Dried sticks gathered together in a bundle, sometimes used to replace the more common wire brush of the percussionist. Edgar Varèse, in his composition *Intégrales* (1925), uses the switch on a bass drum shell to create dry-sounding rhythms.

symbolism: A movement starting around 1888 that came in reaction to impressionism*and realism. Symbolism sought to suggest states of mind, moods, and concepts through the use of decorative forms and pictorial symbols. The movement was a loosely-knit one, and artists such as Georges Rouault, Maurice Denis, and Odilon Redon are often identified with symbolism in addition to the primary figure of Paul Gauguin.

symmetrical chord: See reflective* chord.

symmetrical formation: A harmonic structure or progression in which one half is an exact inversion of the other half. See reflective* chord, symmetrical* scale.

symmetrical scale: A synthetic* scale in which the lower tetrachord* is an inversion* of the upper tetrachord.

symmetrical series: A twelve-tone* row or fragment of a row in which one segment is an inversion*, retrograde*, retrograde-inversion*, or transposition* of another segment. For example, the second hexachord* of a row might be an inversion of the first hexachord. See derivation* technique.

synch: Abbreviation for synchronize or synchronization.

synthesizer: A system of electronic instruments that may be interconnected in various ways to produce sounds. Three basic classes of equipment are generally used: (1) oscillators* and random* generators, (2) filters*, and (3) amplitude* processors (envelope* generators, voltage-controlled* amplifiers). The operator is able to produce and vary the frequency*, amplitude*, and timbre* of sounds through various kinds of controllers*. Synthesizers are used to duplicate the sounds of musical instruments and to create new sounds for electronic* music.

synthetic music: See coded-performance* music.

synthetic scale: Generally this term has been applied to any scale other than traditional major and minor and the ancient church modes. However, the inclusion of folk scales or scales from music of non-Western cultures under this heading has been questioned by some scholars. See enigmatic* scale, Prometheus* scale, symmetrical* scale, two-octave* scale, gapped* scale, hexatonic* scale, double* harmonic scale, overtone* scale, major* Locrian scale, Lydian* minor scale.

T

T: Abbreviation for transposed or transposition*. The letter T is used to identify a twelve-tone* row or a segment of a row that has been moved to a new pitch level.

tachism: See action* painting.

tag ending: A codetta present in jazz* that brings the performance of a work to a close. Sometimes tag endings involve short bits of improvisation* by each player in turn before the final close.

tailgate: Parades in New Orleans often had a jazz* band located on a flat wagon or back of a truck as the parade moved through town. The trombonist would usually sit at the back of the wagon so that he could use his slide unhampered by obstacle. The long trombone glissandi associated with such performances became known as tailgate.

tango: A ballroom dance in 4/4 meter of Argentine origin. The dance in its native South American state was considered too seamy and suggestive for European audiences and a refined version was introduced to the continent by the Frenchman Camille de Rhymal in 1907. By 1914 the dance had spread to the United States. The dance pattern involved two slow steps, two quick steps, and one slow step (the quick steps being twice as fast as the slow steps).

It was called "baile con corte" (dance with a stop) in Argentina. The tango has had influence on some American popular music as witnessed by a work such as *Blue Tango* (1951) by Leroy Anderson.

tape: See magnetic* tape.

tape bins: A storage rack for magnetic* tape.

tape cartridge: A plastic container for a length of magnetic* tape designed to make manual threading unnecessary. The tape in the cartridge is usually in the form of an endless loop that feeds out through the center of a reel and back to the outside. Tape cartridges are used most frequently in automobile playback* systems. See cassette*.

tape cassette: See cassette*.

tape deck: A tape* recorder that usually does not include a preamplifier*, amplifier*, or loudspeakers*. Tape decks are used in larger electronic systems where these other instruments are available as separate components.

tape head: See record* head, playback* head, erase* head.

tape hiss: Undesirable random noise that is either inherent on magnetic* tape or a by-product of tape* recording.

tape loop: A circular piece of magnetic* tape used to create ostinato* pitch and rhythm patterns in electronic* music.

tape machine: See tape* recorder.

tape magazine: See cassette*, tape* cartridge.

tape manipulation: The processes involved in working directly with prerecorded magnetic* tape (containing sounds from conventional musical sources, the environment, electronic instruments, etc.) and tape* recorders in the production of materials for electronic* music and musique* concrète. Techniques such as reversing ʻthe direction of the tape, splicing from one tape onto another, altering tape speed, and creating tape* loops are characteristic.

tape music: Music in which tape* manipulation is used in the compositional process. Techniques such as reversing the direction of the tape, splicing tape fragments, superimposing sounds from one tape onto another, altering tape speed, and creating tape* loops are commonly employed. Musique* concrète and electronic* music fall into the category of tape music, which as an identifying term is falling into disuse.

tape recorder: An electronic device which converts sound into electrical energy for storage on magnetic* tape and then reconverts the electrical energy into sound. Microphones* translate sounds into fluctuating voltages* which are fed to record* heads. The record heads produce magnetic fields which rearrange the metallic-oxide particles suspended on magnetic tape into corresponding patterns. When sound retrieval is desired, playback* heads reconvert the patterns on magnetic tape into fluxuating voltages which are translated into actual sounds by amplifiers* and loudspeakers*. See quarter-track* tape recorder, full-track* tape recorder, two-track* tape recorder, four-track* tape recorder, multiple-track* tape recorder.

tape recorder music: See tape* music.

tape recording: The process of storing audio* or video* information on magnetic* tape for retrieval at a later time. See tape* recorder, tape* music, tape* manipulation.

tape studio: A studio where recordings on magnetic* tape are made.

tape transport: That part of a tape* deck that holds the reels and moves the magnetic* tape past the record* and erase* heads.

Teiler: A dominant chord that is used as a structural divider in Schenkerian* analysis or one that prolongs a basic underlying tone. See prolongation*.

telescoping: A term sometimes applied to notes of a tone* row simultaneously used in different voices, producing harmony from their verticalization*.

telharmonium: An early electronic* musical instrument, first demonstrated in 1903, of gigantic size, weighing over two hundred tons! It produced music by means of dynamos running on alternating current and transmitted the electrically-generated music to the public over telephone wires. Thaddeus Cahill, the inventor of the machine, hoped to have paid subscribers who would have the music of the telharmonium piped into their homes, hotels, or restaurants.

tempo clicks: See warning* clicks.

tempo modulation: See metrical* modulation.

tempophone: A tape* recording device that allows either pitch or performance speed to remain constant while the other is altered. See Zeitdehner*.

temporal saturation: A term from the Schillinger* system used to denote a situation in which thematic groups enter at an ever-increasing rate. The term is roughly synonymous with the conventional concept of stretto.

terminal: 1. A device used to transmit and receive information in a computer* or other communication system. **2.** A device found at the end of an electrical wire that functions as a connector into a circuit*.

tertial harmony: See tertian* harmony.

tertian harmony: Chord construction in thirds as in triads, seventh chords, ninth* chords, eleventh* chords, thirteenth* chords.

tetrachord: 1. Four adjacent notes of a set* or row* in twelve-tone* music, especially the first, second, or third group within the group of twelve. (See example a.) 2. The term is also applied to any consecutive four note segment of a diatonic scale. (See example b.)

tetrad: 1. A vertical* sonority consisting of four different pitches. 2. The simultaneous sounding of an unordered* four note set*.

theatre of the absurd: An avant-garde* style of theatrical presentation in which the conventional concepts of theme, plot, and character are ignored or distorted and irrationality and man's isolation in the world are stressed. Theatre of the absurd has had a great influence on the development of aleatoric* music and is often combined with other elements in multimedia* presentations.

THD: An abbreviation for total harmonic distortion, including both artificial overtones* and hum*.

theory of games: See game* theory.

theremin: A monophonic* electronic* musical instrument invented by the Russian scientist Leon Theremin around 1924. Pitch is controlled by moving the hand near a metal rod which is connected to a variable-frequency oscillator*. A second oscillator operates at a fixed frequency* and the combination of the two frequencies produces a third beat-frequency which is transmitted to a loudspeaker*. Another metal rod is used in similar fashion by the other hand to control loudness. The result is a free sound much like that of a musical saw. Among a number

of composers who have utilized the theremin are Joseph Schillinger who wrote *First Airplane Suite* for theremin and orchestra in 1929 and Miklos Rosza who used the theremin in the film scores for *Spellbound* and *Lost Weekend* in the 1940's.

thereminovox: See etherophone*.

thermal notes: See white* noise.

third order set: A term originated by composer and theorist Milton Babbitt to designate a source* set that creates combinatorial relationships at three different levels of transposition*. See combinatoriality*.

third stream: Jazz* music that incorporates elements of the "serious" or "classical" idiom (particularly contemporary trends such as serialism* and modality*) or concert music influenced by jazz*. It is difficult to indicate the precise balance that is required between jazz and "serious" music to qualify a work as third stream. Generally, a spirit of experimentation is present in such pieces, and often a more cerebral attitude toward the aesthetic whole is found than in the average jazz composition. Although the idea of such an amalgam is not unique to the second half of the twentieth century (the music of George Gershwin, Claude Debussy's *Golliwog's Cakewalk* [1906], Stravinsky's *Ragtime* [1918] and *Histoire du Soldat* [1918], Darius Milhaud's *La Création du Monde* [1923], Ernst Krenek's *Jonny Spielt Auf* [1927], Kurt Weill's *Three Penny Opera* [1928], and Alban Berg's *Lulu* [1937] all contain jazz elements) it is composers and performers such as Gunther Schuller (*Seven Studies on Themes of Paul Klee* [1959]), Milton Babbitt (*All Set* [1957]), and Dave Brubeck (*The Light in the Wilderness* [1968]) who are generally regarded as third stream figures of importance. The term itself was coined by Gunther Schuller.

thirteenth chord: A tertian* sonority with a basic structure consisting of seven different notes. It can be viewed as a combination of three triads with tones in common at two points.

thirteenth tone: A term used by composer John Cage to refer to silence.

three dimensional wand: A potentiometer* that can control three different elements.

thunderstick: See bull* roarer.

timbre: The particular quality or color of a sound which results from a specific relationship of the amplitudes* and frequencies* of its component waveforms*. Timbre has become a very important element in twentieth century music both in its relationship to traditional musical instruments (see Klangfarbenmelodie*) and to the infinite possibilities of electronic* music.

timbre modulation: The process of changing the tone color of a sound by altering the frequencies* and amplitudes* of its component waveforms*. See electronic* music.

time-field: A rhythmic pattern, or subdivision of a rhythmic pattern which is difficult to perform because of its complexity and lack of immediate relation to the overriding metric structure. A rhythm such as the one indicated below would be an example of a time-field.

time-point set: A term employed by theorist-composer Milton Babbitt to indicate the serial ordering of rhythmic and metric units derived from the intervallic structure of a given set*. The pitch* number of the set is interpretable as the point of initiation of a temporal event*, as it is assigned a metric value. The result is that a serialization* of meter occurs.

time-sharing: An access system that allows a number of individuals to utilize a computer* concurrently. Time-sharing is possible because of the extremely high speed (in relation to man's ability to think and react) of present-day computers.

time-stretcher: See Zeitdehner*.

tin pan alley: Various districts in New York City where popular music is published. The first district was located around 28th Street and 6th Avenue. Publishing houses such as T. B. Harms; M. Witmark and Sons; Shapiro, Bernstein, and Von Tilzer; and Marks and Stern were located there. The area later moved uptown to 32nd Street and later yet to the Times Square area from 42nd Street to 50th Street. The name itself probably derives from the sound of tinny rehearsal pianos clinking away in these establishments.

tone-cluster: A sonority produced by the simultaneous striking of notes at the interval of a second. A tone-cluster may be easily produced by striking the keyboard with a forearm or flattened hand, a technique often found in the piano music of Charles Ives, Henry Cowell, and Béla Bartók. Cowell is generally considered to be the composer who has exploited tone-clusters most thoroughly in his music. Different methods of notation have been devised. If a cluster is a small one, all of the tones are generally written in conventional notation. For larger clusters a bar-like design is often found, as in example (a) below. If a cluster is desired on the black keys of the piano, a sharp or flat sign is placed beside the cluster, as in example (b).

tone poem: A symphonic work, usually in one movement, that attempts to depict a visual, poetic, or literary idea in music. The rather free approach to form in the tone poem, along with the fact that it has extramusical connotations, makes it an important form with evolutionary significance for twentieth century composers. In the hands of Franz Liszt (*Les Préludes* [1854]), Richard Strauss (*Till Eulenspiegel* [1895]), and Claude Debussy (*Prélude à l'Après-midi d'un Faune* [1892-4]) the tone poem reached its apex in the latter half of the nineteenth century. Some later composers who have carried on the tradition of the tone poem include Arthur Honegger (*Pacific 231* [1924]), Charles Ives (*Central Park in the Dark* [1898-1907]), Igor Stravinsky (*Rite of Spring* [1913]), and Aaron Copland (*Appalachian Spring* [1944]).

tone row: An ordering of pitches in a particular sequence that becomes the basis for a given melodic or harmonic structure. A tone row may be comprised of any number of tones according to the intent of the composer, but the twelve-tone* row is by far the most common.

tonicalization: A term in Schenkerian* analysis for the internal weight and structural significance that subordinate musical strata (i.e., middleground* events) assume in the overall coherence of a given work, particularly in regard to the fundamental governing structures (i.e., background*).

tonicization: A term used by composer Roger Sessions to indicate a process whereby harmonic cells in tonal music are established with less weight than they would be through modulation, but are nevertheless transient focal points of key center. Usually, such progressions involve the use of secondary dominant (applied dominant) relationships in order to become established. Modulation means a real change of key; tonicization may be thought of as internal focus on harmonic centers without the more prolonged preparation required by modulation. Sessions claims that tonicization is an Anglicized form of the German word Tonikalisierung coined by Heinrich Schenker.

tonlos: A term that designates a whispered tone, usually notated by the symbol indicated below. Arnold Schoenberg is credited with the invention of the tonlos, and other composers (e.g., Luciano Berio in *Circles* [1960]) have employed it also.

Tonorten: A German term that corresponds to pitch* classes.

Tonreihe: Geman for tone* row.

total control: A term used to indicate music in which all parameters* are pre-arranged. Serialization is applied to pitch, rhythm, dynamics, articulation, texture, and register. A good example of a work using this procedure is *Structures I* (1952) by Pierre Boulez. Often difficult for the uninitiated to follow, totally controlled works sometimes give an impression of a lack of organization or structure, perhaps because each of the musical elements tends to receive equal attention in the composition. See serial* music.

total organization: See total* control.

total predetermination: See total* control.

total serialization: See total* control.

track: A specific and continuous area of magnetic* tape or film which contains recorded information derived from a single electronic channel*. See tape* recorder, multiple-track* recording.

transducer: A device that transforms one kind of energy into another kind. For example, a loudspeaker* which transforms electrical energy into sound* waves.

transformation: 1. The changing of one form, element, characteristic, or structure into another. 2. One of the three basic rearrangements of a twelve-tone* row (whose original form is called the prime*). Inversion* is the row stated with its intervals constructed in the opposite vertical direction, retrograde* is the row stated backwards, and retrograde-inversion* is the row stated backwards and in the opposite vertical direction. The following tone row transformations are from Arnold Schoenberg's *Third Quartet*, Op. 30 (1927).

transformer: A device that transfers electrical energy from one circuit* to another. In the process the frequency* remains the same but the voltage* usually changes. Transformers are important components in much electronic sound producing and modifying equipment including amplifiers* and synthesizers*.

transient generator: An electronic device used to duplicate the attack* sounds of musical instruments. See

envelope* generator, transient* overtones.

transient overtones: Partials* which rapidly diminish in intensity as in the attack* phase of a musical instrument such as a piano. Transient overtones are an important consideration when sounds are being created or duplicated with a synthesizer*.

transient response: The ability of an electronic device to respond clearly and rapidly to sudden and brief signals* such as those found in percussive sounds.

transients: See transient* overtones.

transistor: An electronic device used in a circuit* to amplify, or modify in some other way, the flow of current*. Transistors are an important component of most electronic equipment including amplifiers*, synthesizers*, and computers*. See solid-state*.

transposition: The movement of a group of notes to a different pitch level while keeping the interval relationships exactly the same. Transposition is an integral part of the compositional process in twelve-tone* technique.

transpositional number: The integer* assigned to designate the interval of transposition* of a tone* row. 0 implies no transposition. Hence P0 indicates the prime* form of a row nontransposed. The number 1 represents a transposition one half-step above the original*, 2 represents two half-steps above the original, and so forth. Transpositional numbers are used in conjunction with pitch* numbers to arrive at transposed forms of a row quickly. For example, a row represented by the following pitch numbers – 0, 7, 9, 2, 11, 4, 6, 1, 8, 3, 10, 5 – can readily be transposed a perfect fourth above by adding 5 to each number – 5, 0, 2, 7, 4, 9, 11, 6, 1, 8, 3, 10. Note that where the resulting sum is 12 or more, 12 must be deducted as it represents duplication at the octave.

trautonium: A monophonic* electronic* musical instrument invented by the German engineer Friedrich Trautwein first demonstrated in Berlin in 1930. The sound of the earliest trautonium was produced by means of a neon tube. In later models the neon tube was replaced by a gas triode. Pitch on the trautonium is controlled by one or two keyboards but can be made continuously variable by moving the keys sideways. Various modes of attack are possible, depending on finger pressure, and loudness is controlled with a foot pedal. Formant* circuits* produce a variety of timbres*. Paul Hindemith wrote *Studies for Three Trautoniums* (1930) and *Concertino for Trautonium* (1931). In 1940 Richard Strauss used the trautonium in *Japanese Festival Music*. See mixturtrautonium*.

triangular wave: A waveform* containing the fundamental frequency* and odd numbered harmonics* which decrease in amplitude* rapidly in relation to their distance from the fundamental*. In this waveform the voltage* ascends at a constant rate of change to positive and then suddenly descends at the same rate to negative, producing the following visual pattern on an oscilloscope*.

trichord: 1. Any combination of three pitches heard as a chord. 2. Three adjacent notes in a tone* row.

trigger: A signal* used to initiate an electronic process such as the switching on or off of an oscillator* in a synthesizer*.

trigger delay: An electronic device that accepts a trigger* voltage* and then, after a designated time (us-

ually from .002 to 10 seconds), produces a control voltage.

trigram: A symbol consisting of three whole or divided lines used in ancient Chinese and Japanese divination. A trigram can also be considered as half of a hexagram*. See *I Ching**.

tritone: Three whole-tones constituting the interval of a diminished fifth or an augmented fourth. Chords built using tritones and melodies employing important tritone configurations are notable in much twentieth century music because of the potential the interval holds for tonal vagueness.

trope: The name given to the basic tone* row structures in the twelve-tone* system of theorist and composer Josef Hauer as described in his book *Zwölftontechnik* (1926). Each of Hauer's forty-four different possible tropes is conceived as a combination of two hexachords* of different pitch content in which all twelve notes of the chromatic scale are present. The pitches within each hexachord are significant in content but not in order of succession. The composer is free to utilize the pitches of each hexachord in any order he desires. Hauer's tropes are similar in concept to Milton Babbitt's source* sets in that they both generate pitch relationships for compositional use and hence serve as unifying systems for twelve-tone works.

tuner: An electronic device that converts radio broadcasts into audio* signals*.

turnback: A connecting chord progression in jazz*, usually two measures in length, that leads back to the start of the tune. Some basic turnbacks follow:

C	A7	D 7	G7 ‖
Em7	Am7	Dm7	G7 ‖
CM7	Bb7	Ab 7	G7 ‖
CM7	Eb7	Ab 7	Db 7‖

turntable: A revolving platform on which phonograph records are placed for recording or playback*.

tweeter: A small loudspeaker* that reproduces the higher frequency* sound waves. See woofer*.

twelve-note music: A British term for twelve-tone* music.

twelve-note chord: A chord containing all twelve notes of the chromatic scale. Twelve-note chords can be constructed in thirds (see example a), seconds (see example b), fourths (see example c), as polychords*, as reflective* chords, or according to other organizational systems including twelve-tone* technique.

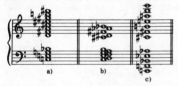

a)   b)   c)

twelve-tone music: See twelve-tone* technique.

twelve-tone row: The twelve chromatic tones within an octave arranged in a given sequence. While a twelve-tone row can contain any succession of pitches, most twelve-tone composers have chosen to design rows that utilize intervallic relationships devoid of a sense of key or tonal center. It is important to note that a tone row is an ordering of tones from which the composer draws pitch material. It has no rhythmic or melodic life of its own. It does not control the composition itself. The tone row has four basic forms (which are described and illustrated under transformation*). See twelve-tone* music, serialized* harmony, serialized* melody.

twelve-tone technique: A term generally reserved for the system of musical composition developed by Arnold Schoenberg around 1923-1924. The following principles are involved: 1. the twelve chromatic tones within an octave are arranged in a sequence with no tone repeated; 2. the row has four basic forms — original*, inversion*, retrograde*, and retrograde-inversion* (see example under transformation); 3. the row structure is to remain constant throughout the composition, allowing for octave* equivalence and for transpositions* of any of the basic forms listed under 2 above; 4. the tones of the row may be made into chords (see serialized* harmony) or melodic patterns (see serialized* melody); 5. octave doublings of pitches are to be avoided. It is to be stressed that the above "rules" are useful only insofar as they lend themselves to the artistic gift of a composer. Many composers have taken liberties with these basic premises when they have felt that their immediate musical purposes have required certain flexibilities and freedom. See appendix under twelve-tone technique for all related terms contained in this volume.

twenty-third chord: A twelve-note chord such as the one illustrated below. While such chords are theoretically possible, they are rarely found in music because of their extreme density and lack of tonal direction.

two-octave scale: A scale so constructed that the starting note does not reappear until two octaves of pitches have been stated.

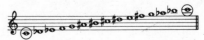

two-track tape recorder: A tape* recorder in which two channels* of information are usually recorded on one-quarter inch magnetic* tape. The two tracks* cover the width of the tape with only a slight space between, and both channels are recorded in the same direction. Sometimes two-track tape recorders are referred to as half-track tape recorders. See four-track* tape recorder, multi-track* tape recorder.

two-voice framework: A term from Hindemith's *Craft of Musical Composition* (1941) that refers to the governing melodic contour of the bass voice and the most important upper voice. The melodic framework contributes to harmonic development. If the bass is a pedal-point, the next voice above it will be the lower half of the two-voice framework, and if the upper voice holds one tone for an extended time period the next lowest voice becomes the upper member of the framework. Hindemith maintains that if a work of any complexity is to result, the two-voice framework must be well-organized and virtually able to stand on its own.

typophone: See dulcitone*.

U

Uebertragung der Ursatzformer: An internal repetition in Schenkerian* analysis that duplicates, in smaller detail, the larger or more fundamental melodic motion of the background* or middleground*.

undecad: A vertical* sonority consisting of eleven different pitches.

undertone series: An inversion* of the intervals of the overtone (harmonic*) series.

unequal rhythmic groups: A combination of two different rhythmic groups such as two against three (example a); three against four (example b); or seven against three (example c).

uni-directional: A term usually used in conjunction with a microphone* that picks up sound from one direction only.

unmeasured meter: See variable* meter.

unordered pitch classes: A collection of three or more notes in a twelve-tone* work in which each note is from a different pitch* class with no specified succession. For example, the occurrence of E, Bb, F as E, F, Bb, or F, E, Bb or as a vertical* sonority in which no succession is evident. See ordered* pitch classes, unordered* set, trope*, aggregate*.

unordered set: A collection of notes with no specified succession. A twelve-tone* row that functions as an unordered set will not be subjected to retrograde* because a specific succession of notes in the original* would have to be assumed. An unordered set includes the total pitch content of a passage or work without regard to the precise sequence of notes. See set*, ordered* set.

Unterbrechung: German for "interruption" as used in Schenkerian* analysis. An interruption is a break in the musical structure (indicated in a Schenkerian graph by the symbol

||). Movement to a half cadence on V is typical of the kind of harmonic pause that helps to create an interruption.

urbanism: See machine* music.

Urlinie: The fundamental line in Schenkerian* analysis, meaning the primary or overall directionality exhibited by the melodic lines in a work, primarily in the upper voices. The Urlinie is indicated in either of two ways: (1) with numerals standing for corresponding scale degrees; or (2) with a beam that connects the stemmed open-headed notes.

Ursatz: A term from Schenkerian* analysis that refers to the contrapuntal structure resulting from the coordination of the Urlinie* and the Grundbrechung*.

V

vagrant harmonies: Arnold Schoenberg's term for equivocal chords such as the diminished seventh, half-diminished seventh, and augmented sixth. These chords have a multiple meaning, because they can move to a number of possible harmonic goals or resolutions.

valeurs ajoutees: See added* value.

vamp: A passage of indefinite length in jazz* or popular music used to prepare for the entrance of a soloist (e.g., singer) or to provide a continuous chordal background over which a soloist might improvise.

variable meter: Rapid metric changes with no consistent pattern of repetition.

$$\frac{|3}{|4} \quad \frac{|5}{|8} \quad \frac{|6}{|4} \quad \frac{|2}{|1} \quad \frac{|3}{|8} \text{ etc:}$$

variable speed unit: A device used to alter and control the speed at which magnetic* tape passes across the heads* of a tape* recorder. Manipulation of tape speed by means of a variable speed unit is a frequently-

used technique in the composition of electronic* music.

variable transformer: A transformer* with provision for varying output* voltage* within a specified range.

variac: The trade name for a specific variable* transformer.

VCA: See voltage-controlled* amplifier.

VCF: See voltage-controlled* filter.

VCO: See voltage-controlled* oscillator.

verism: The concept that the subject matter for works of art can be commonplace, coarse, or even repugnant and still have aesthetic validity. Both painting and opera, which had been characterized in earlier times by beautiful, noble, and legendary themes, moved strongly toward verism in the early twentieth century. See veristic* surrealism.

veristic surrealism: A post-World War I art movement characterized by dream-like images rendered with photographic precision. Dali, Tanguy, and Ernst were active in this style of painting. See verism*, surrealism*.

verse: The introduction to the main body or chorus of a popular song. The verse is usually shorter (eight to sixteen measures is a typical length) than the chorus and has the function of setting the scene for the subject of the chorus. Verses are seldom found in recent popular songs.

verticalization: The concept that any group of notes that has significance as a linear succession will also have significance as a vertical* sonority. Chord structures in twelve-tone* technique are generally the result of verticalization. This concept is also referred to as vertical melody.

vertical melody: See verticalization*.

vertical permutation: The "harmonic" or vertical inversion* (as opposed to linear or horizontal inversion*) of a simultaneous statement of a portion of a twelve-tone* row. Example (a) below indicates a simultaneity* and example (b) its vertical permutation:

a) 𝄢 ... b) 𝄢 ...

vertical sonority: Any combination of notes sounded simultaneously. This term, along with a number of others (see simultaneity*, note* complex, vertical* melody), has been used to replace the term "chord", which to many implies a traditional harmonic structure in thirds.

vibes: See vibraphone*.

vibraharp: See vibraphone*.

vibraphone: A percussion instrument common to jazz* and occasionally used by "serious" contemporary composers (e.g., Alban Berg in *Lulu* [1937], Pierre Boulez in *Improvisation sur Mallarmé* [1958]) that has an aluminum keyboard with a range of three octaves. The bars of the keyboard have metal resonators below, and the tops of the resonators are equipped with discs that revolve by electrical power, creating a vibrato effect (although the instrument can be used with or without the vibrato by switching the motor off). The jazz idiom has a number of vibraphone virtuosi including Gary McFarland, Lionel Hampton, Milt Jackson, and Red Norvo.

vibrations per second: See hertz*.

video: A term that pertains to the electronic transmission of visual information. Video, which is Latin for "I see", is primarily associated with television, which on occasion is involved in multimedia* presentations.

vocoder: An electronic device originally designed to encode speech sounds into digital* signals for transmission by radio or communication cable. Composers have used the vocoder

to create new sounds through the modification of existing sounds.

voltage: The force that causes electrical energy to move through a system.

voltage control: The use of an externally applied voltage* to control the operating characteristics of an electronic instrument. See voltage-controlled* amplifier, voltage-controlled* filter, voltage-controlled* oscillator.

voltage-controlled amplifier: An amplifier* in which the amplitude* of a signal* being processed can be controlled by an externally applied voltage*.

voltage-controlled filter: A filter* in which the cutoff frequency* can be controlled by an externally applied voltage*.

voltage-controlled oscillator: An oscillator* in which the waveform* frequency* can be carried by an externally applied voltage*.

Vordergrund: German for foreground* as used in Schenkerian* analysis.

vps: Abbreviation for vibrations per second. See hertz*.

VU meter: A device common to amplifiers* and mixers* which indicates visually the decibel* level of the signals* being processed.

W

wah-wah: 1. A jazz* effect in which the musician makes an approximation of the syllables "wah-wah" on his instrument. The wah-wah, or "laughing" sound, is typically performed by brass players. Often a mute or rubber plunger (called a wow-wow or wah-wah mute) is utilized to create this effect. The wah-wah is notated as indicated below.

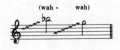
(wah - wah)

2. A type of electronic sound common to rock* music achieved by rocking a pedal volume control.

walking bass: A pizzicato jazz* bass line that moves in steady quarter-notes combining scale patterns with broken chord formations. Non-harmonic passing tones are very common in this type of bass pattern.

wallpaper music: 1. Music that repeats incessantly until it recedes into the background soundscape*. Erik Satie's *Vexations* (1892-3), a short work for piano that repeats over and over, making a particular point of the boring repetition, might be considered a work of this genre. **2.** The term is also applied to "background" music such as Muzak* that one hears in department stores and airports.

warning clicks: A click* track that precedes the first measure of a segment of music on a motion picture sound* track and is used to prepare the composer or conductor by setting the tempo of the music to follow.

waveform: The visual representation of a sound wave showing amplitude* versus time. See sine* wave, square* wave, triangular* wave, pulse* wave, sawtooth* wave.

weighted noise: See colored* noise.

weighted sound: See colored* noise.

whang gun: See spoils* of war.

white noise: A pitchless, non-repetitive signal* containing all audible frequencies* with randomly varying but relatively equal amplitudes*. The sound of white noise is like rushing air or escaping steam and is used as a common sound source in electronic* music. See colored* noise, pink* noise, blue* noise, random* generator.

white noise generator: See random* generator.

white-note collection: Melodic and harmonic structures that utilize the white keys of the piano. See pandiatonicism*.

white-sound: See white* noise.

white tone: Synonymous with non-vibrato, this effect is common in much contemporary music.

whole-tone chord: A chord comprised of six (or less) tones of a whole-tone* scale.

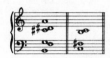

whole-tone dominant: A dominant chord built from the tones of the whole-tone* scale. All six tones may be used (example a), or the chord may employ fewer than six (example b) and still retain a strong dominant feeling.

whole-tone scale: A scale consisting of six whole-tones to the octave. The whole-tone scale has a nebulous tonal feeling due to the lack of a dominant, subdominant, and leading tone function and contains the interval of a tritone* from the first note of the scale to the fourth. Although the scale has primarily been employed by twentieth century composers such as Béla Bartók, Charles Ives, Erik Satie and Igor Stravinsky it was used, somewhat experimentally, by earlier composers such as Franz Liszt, Michael Glinka, and Vladimir Rebikov.

wideband response: The generally consistent amplitude* response of an electronic device over a large range of frequencies*.

wild: The recording of film* music under the control of a stopwatch rather than by direct visual coordination with the motion picture.

wind machine: A device used to imitate the rushing of wind. A barrel-shaped frame is covered with cloth or silk, which, when turned rapidly rubs against the wood creating the wind sound. Richard Strauss has used this effect in *Don Quixote* (1898) and the *Alpine Symphony* (1915), Maurice Ravel used it in *Daphnis et Chloé* (1912), and Ralph Vaughan Williams employed it in his *Sinfonia Antartica* (1951-2).

wind sound sculpture: A sculpture designed so that it creates some kind of sound when the wind passes over or through it.

woofer: A loudspeaker* designed to handle the lower frequencies* in sound reproduction.

wow: Pitch distortion, usually in the form of minute fluctuations or waverings caused by uneven turntable* or tape* recorder speed.

wrong note harmonization: The use of chords deliberately conceived to sound "wrong" or inappropriate in order to achieve a musical affect of humor or parody. A good example of such a musical passage is the *Polka* from the ballet *The Golden Age* (1930) by Dimitri Shostakovich.

X

xyloflux: A modern harp technique similar to the oboic* flux in which a glissando with the fingernails is utilized close to the sounding board. The xyloflux is indicated in the following manner:

xylomarimba: A large xylophone often found in contemporary scores (e.g., Karlheinz Stockhausen's *Gruppen* (1959) and Pierre Boulez's *Le Mar-*

teau sans Maître [1955]) that covers the ranges of both the xylophone and marimba.

xylorimba: See xylomarimba*.

Y

yang: In Chinese philosophy yang and yin are polar opposites represented graphically by ☯ . This image stands for the forces that continually are at work changing the universe and they constantly interact with each other. Yang is considered to be a male element, the source of heat, life, and light. Yin represents the female element to which cold, darkness, and death are ascribed. Some contemporary composers who have studied Oriental philosophy have been influenced by these concepts and have incorporated them in various ways into their musical thinking.

Yi King: See *I Ching**.

yin: See yang*.

Z

Zeitdehner: An electronic device capable of altering the playback* speed of recorded material without affecting the frequency* or vice versa.

Zen philosophy: A branch of Buddhist philosophy that places an emphasis on mysticism, ultimate insight (sartori), contemplative and intuitive thinking, a denial of ordinary logic, a love of nature, and the importance of personal integrity. The Zen movement has had a great influence on certain American composers such as John Cage, Morton Feldman, and Earle Brown.

zug: A term common in Schenkerian* analysis that denotes linear progression such as movement through the interval of a third (Terzzug) or a sixth (Sextzug), etc. See Schenkerian* analysis.

APPENDIX
A Topical Listing of the Terms Included in This Dictionary

Abbreviations
A
AM
ASCAP
bit
BMI
BTL
cps
db
DC
DI
DIC
DS
FM
H⁻
HR
Hz
I
IO
ISCM
IT
kHz
N⁻
NC
NI
NS
O
OT
P
PC
PI
pot
R
R and B
RI
RIT
RT
S
synch
T
THD
VCA
VCF
VCO
vps

Art Movements
abstract art
abstract expressionism

action painting
antirealistic art
art deco
art nouveau
bruitism
constructivism
cubism
dada
environmental art
exoticism
expressionism
fauvism
fiber sculpture
formalism
futurism
geometric abstraction
hai-ku
impressionism
kinetic art
kitsch
Kulturbolschevismus
magic realism
mechanistic aesthetic
minimal art
mixed-media art
multimedia art
neo-classicism
neo-impressionism
neo-romanticism
non-objective art
objectivism
op art
oscilloscopic art
pointillism
pop art
primitive art
psychedelic art
rayonism
realism
realistic sculpture
referentialism
retinal art
sharp-focus realism
social realism
surrealism
symbolism
tachism
theatre of the absurd
urbanism

verism
veristic surrealism
wind sound sculpture
Also see listings under **Musical Styles.**

Chance Music
aleatory
Book of Changes
chance music
chance operations
chronometer
coins technique
event
game theory
hexagram
I Ching
imperfections technique
improvisation
indeterminacy
interchangeability
kua
Monte Carlo method
note field
probability theory
random music
stochastic music
strategic music
trigram
Also see listings
   under **Multimedia.**

Compositional Techniques
athematicism
atonalism
augmentation
bimodality
bitonality
cancrizans
circular permutation
collage
controlled improvisation
counterchord
diminution
diodic texture
dismemberment
dissonant counterpoint
dual modality
escaped chord
evaporation
Fortspinnung
fragmentation
harmonic crescendo

harmonic diminuendo
harmonic litany
harmonic planes
harmonic synthesis
heterophony
improvisation
Inselbildung
interval variation
inversion
involution
isomelos
isorhythm
isotrophy
Klangfarben technique
layering
liquidation
magic square
metamorphosis
microtonalism
millimetration
mirror
modal interchange
modality
modal modulation
montage
ostinato
palindrome
pandiatonicism
paper flyspeck
parallel harmony
parallelism
passive resolution
perpetual variation
planing
pointal imperfection
pointillism
polytonality
prepared piano
projection
pyramids
quartal harmony
quarter-tone
retrograde
retrograde-inversion
retrogression
root clouding
Schillinger system
speech melody
Sprechgesang
Sprechstimme
superimposition
temporal saturation

tonicization
transformation
transposition
white-note collection
wrong note harmonization
Also see listings under **Chance Music,
Computer Music, Electronic Music
Synthesis, Film Music, Harmonic Resources, Jazz and Popular Music,
Multimedia, Musical Styles, Performance Practices, Rhythm and Meter,
Scale Resources, Set Theory and
Twelve-tone Music.**

Computer Music
ALGOL
algorithm
alphanumeric notation
analog computer
analog signal
analog tape
analog to digital conversion
analog to digital converter
analysis-synthesis
BASIC
Bell Laboratories
binary digit
binary input language
bit
BTL system
buffer
byte
CALCOMP
card punch
closed loop
COBOL
code
coding
compiler
computer
computer music
conditional transfer
CSL system
cybernetics
DARMS
data card
debug
digital computer
digital signal
digital tape
digital to analog conversion
digital to analog converter

direct access
disk file
disk pack
disk storage
entropy
flip-flop
flow chart
Ford-Columbia representation
FORTRAN
game theory
hard copy
hardware
ILLIAC computer
IML
information theory
interface
keypunch
machine language
Markoff chain music
Markoff process
memory
MIR
Monte Carlo method
MUSIC
MUSICOMP
MUSTUD
operation
optical scanner
order code
output
paper-tape programmer
paper-tape reader
print-out
program
programming
programming **language**
punch card
random access
random number generator
real time
relay
RILM
routine
scaling
SERIES
SNOBOL
software
stochastic music
storage
subroutine
terminal
time-sharing

Also see listings under
  Electronic Music Synthesis,
  Electronics and Acoustics,
  Electronic Sound Reproduction.

Electronic Musical Instruments
aetherophone
dynamophone
dynaphone
electric bass
electronic monochord
electronic musical instruments
electronic sackbut
elektrophon
emicon
etherophone
flexatone
Hammond organ
hellertion
kaleidophon
melochord
melodium
mixturtrautonium
novachord
ondes martenot
partiturophon
rhythmicon
semi-acoustical guitar
solovox
sphärophon
telharmonium
theremin
thereminovox
trautonium
Also see **Electronic Music Synthesis,**
  Electronics and Acoustics, Elec-
  tronic Sound Reproduction.

Electronic Music Synthesis
aleatoric modulation
attack
attack generator
attack transients
attenuator
audio frequency spectrum shifter
audulator
auto-polyphony
band-elimination filter
band-pass filter
band-reject filter
band-stop filter
bandwidth

Bell Laboratories
bi-stable oscillator
black sound
blue noise
Bode melochord
Buchla synthesizer
chronometer
clangorous sounds
classical electronic music studio
coded-performance music
colored noise
Columbia-Princeton Electronic Music
  Center
controller
coordinome
cross-coupling
dual ring modulator
dual trigger delay
dynamic envelope control
Eccles-Jordan trigger
electric music
ElectroComp synthesizer
electronic music
electronic music studio
envelope
envelope follower
envelope generator
exclusion filter
filter
fixed band-pass filter
fixed filter bank
flip-flop
formant filter
French National Radio
frequency
frequency band
frequency counter
frequency modulation
frequency shift
frequency shifter
gate
gating
Gaussian noise
generator
Gerausch
hamograph
hertz
heterodyne
high-pass filter
intensity curve
interface
interval ambit

jack
keyboard controller
Klangumwandler
linear controller
live-electronic music
loop
low-pass filter
manual controller
masking
mixer
mixing
modifier
modular electronic system
modulation
modulator
module
Moog synthesizer
morphology
morphophone
multiple-track tape recorder
multi-vibrator
musique concrète
noiseband
noise generator
notch filter
note complex
note mixture
Oberheim music modulator
optical siren
oscillator
paper-tape programmer
paper-tape reader
patch cord
patch panel
phonogene
pink noise
pot
potentiometer
Putney synthesizer
Radio Cologne
random generator
RCA synthesizer
real-time performance
relay
reverberation unit
ribbon controller
ring modulator
sequential controller
signal
sine wave generator
sound synthesis
sound waves

spiral mesh reverberation unit
stirrer
synthesizer
synthetic music
tape loop
tape manipulation
tape recorder
tempophone
terminal
thermal notes
three dimensional wand
timbre modulation
time-stretcher
transient generator
trigger
trigger delay
variable speed unit
variable transformer
vocoder
voltage-controlled amplifier
voltage-controlled filter
voltage-controlled oscillator
VU meter
weighted noise
white noise
white noise generator
Zeitdehner
Also see listings under
     **Computer Music, Electronic
     Musical Instruments, Electronics
     and Acoustics, Electronic Sound Re-
     production.**

Electronics and Acoustics
amplitude
anechoic chamber
aperiodic vibrations
audio
audio spectrum
cacophony
capacitor
circuit
combination tone
complex tone
current
cycle
cycles per second
decay
decibel
delta wave
Doppler effect
echo

electro-acoustics
electrosonics
Fletcher-Munson curve
formant
formant spectrum
Fourier analysis
free resonance
frequency
frequency band
fundamental
harmonic
harmonic analyzer
harmonic distortion
harmonic series
hertz
impulse
inharmonic partial
matrix
non-periodic
oscillograph
oscilloscope
overtone
partial
peak
periodicity
phase
phase-duration
phon
phoneme
phonology
psychoacoustics
pulse wave
ramp wave
rectangular wave
relay
resistor
resultant tone
reverberation unit
sawtooth wave
signal
sine wave
solid-state
sone
sound spectrum
square wave
steady-state
stroboconn
stroboscope
timbre
transducer
transformer
transient overtones

transistor
triangular wave
undertone series
variable transformer
voltage
voltage control
Also see listings under **Computer Music, Electronic Music Synthesis, Electronic Sound Reproduction.**

Electronic Sound Reproduction
ambience
ambient noise
amplifier
amplitude modulation
attenuation
audio
audio spectrum
band
bandwidth
bulk eraser
cartridge
cassette
channel
choir effect
clipping
closed loop
contact mike
coupling
damping
damping factor
Degausser
demagnetizer
direct-wire recording
distortion
Dolby noise reduction system
doubling
drift
dub
dubbing
dub-down
echo chamber
eight-track cartridge tape recorder
equalizer
erase head
feedback
flux
four-track recording
full-track tape recorder
gain
generation
half-track tape recorder

headphones
hertz
high fidelity
hum
impedence
infinite baffle
input
jack
leader tape
leakage
location modulation
loudspeaker
magnetic print-through
magnetic tape
masking
microphone
monaural
monitor head
monophonic sound
multiple-track tape recorder
omni-directional
open reel
output
panning
peak
playback
playback head
potentiometer
preamplifier
print-through
quadraphonic sound
quarter-track tape recorder
record head
reel-to-reel
ringing
RMS power
rumble
self-thread reels
sel-sync
signal
signal-to-noise-ratio
smoothing filter
solid-state
sound-on-sound
spatial modulation
speaker efficiency
splicer
splicing tape
stereo
stereophonic sound
tape
tape bins

tape cassette
tape deck
tape head
tape hiss
tape loop
tape recorder
tape recording
tape studio
tape transport
terminal
track
transient response
tuner
turntable
tweeter
two-track tape recorder
uni-directional
VU meter
wideband response
woofer
wow
Also see listings under
    Electronic Music Synthesis,
    Electronics and Acoustics.

Film Music
bar breakdown
building
click sheet
click track
combine
cross-fade
cut
dead cue
double tracking
drop out
dub
dubbing
dummy
film music
film phonograph
film recorder
intercut
mag
magnetic track
moviola
optical track
overlap
overlay
punches
sneak start
sound track

split channel recording
spotting
squeezing
streamer
sweetener
tempo clicks
warning clicks
wild

Harmonic Resources
added-note chord
added sixth
addition chord
altered chord
bichord
block chords
chord cluster
chord of addition
chord of omission
chord of resonance
chromatic cluster
cluster
cluster chord
counterchord
decad
duodecad
dyad
eleventh chord
fifteenth chord
fourth chord
Grossmutterakkord
harmonic cluster
heptad
hexad
involution
isomeric sonority
isometric sonority
mirror chord
monad
mystic chord
ninth chord
nonad
non-tertian harmony
octad
open chord
panchromatic chord
pentad
polychord
pyramidal chord
quartal harmony
quintal chord
reflective chord

rootless harmony
secundal chord
seventeenth chord
simultaneity
sound mass
super-dominant
symmetrical chord
tertian harmony
tetrad
thirteenth chord
tone-cluster
trichord
twelve-note chord
undecad
vagrant harmonies
verticalization
vertical melody
vertical permutation
vertical sonority
white-note collection
whole-tone chord
whole-tone dominant

Jazz and Popular Music
arrangement
barrelhouse
big band
bluegrass
blues
blues progression
boogaloo
boogie-woogie
bop
bossa nova
break
bridge
cakewalk
cha-cha
changes
charleston
Chicago style
chorus
combo
comping
conga
country and western
crooner
dixieland
doink
double time
East Coast jazz
flatted fifth

fuzz bass
gospel jazz
growl
gutbucket
hard bop
hard rock
head arrangement
head-riff
honky-tonk
hot jazz
improvisation
jazz
jam
jitterbugging
Kansas City style
lead sheet
lick
mambo
modern jazz
motown
muzak
neophonic orchestra
New Orleans style
new wave
off note
oom-pah figuration
out-chorus
pop tune
progressive jazz
ragtime
riff
rip
rock and roll
rhythm and blues
samba
scat singing
shake
sideman
skiffle
smear
sock chorus
soft rock
soul
spill
spiritual
standard tune
stock arrangement
stomp
stop-time
stride piano
swing
tag ending

tailgate
tango
third stream
tin pan alley
turnback
vamp
verse
wah-wah
walking bass
Also see listings under **Performance Practices.**

Multimedia
color organ
happening
inter-media
laser
light show
Lissajous figure
multimedia art
oscilloscopic art
video
wind sound sculpture
Also see listings under **Chance Music, Electronic Music Synthesis, Film Music.**

Musical Analysis
adjacency
arch form
architectonic levels
Ausfaltung
Auskomponierung
auxiliary degree
axis relations
background
Brechung
centric priority
compositional unfolding
density
event
facade design
falsonance
Fernhören
Fibonacci sequence
foreground
Geschlossenheit
Gestalt
Grundbrechung
Grundgestalt
harmonic dualism
harmonic fluctuation
harmonic monism

Hauptstimme
Hintergrund
Höherlegung
horizontalism
interruption
intersection
intertonal gravitation
interval ambit
Keimzelle theory
mese
middleground
Mittelgrund
morphology
musical gesture
mutation
Nebenstimme
neutral triad
note-density
organic scale
parameter
polarity
prolongation
reduction
resistance forms
rotary motion
Schenkerian analysis
Schillinger system
series of acceleration
series I
SHMRG
sonic imperialism
space-time concept
spans of structure
step progression
structural levels
Stufen
suspended tonality
Teiler
tonicalization
tritone
two-voice framework
Uebertragung der Ursatzformer
Unterbrechung
Urlinie
Ursatz
Vordergrund
yang
yin
Zen philosophy
zug
Also see all other listings in this
   appendix.

Musical Notation
action notation
boxes
directive graphics
equiton
exact notation
eye music
frame notation
graph notation
graphic notation
hinweisende notation
implicit musical graphics
indicative notation
Klavarscribo
musical graphics
qualitative notation

Musical Styles
absolute music
acid rock
anhemitonic music
antimusic
atonality
atonicality
Augenmusik
avant-garde
barrelhouse
bimodality
bitonality
bluegrass
boogie-woogie
bop
bossa nova
Chicago style
computational music
country and western
dixieland
East Coast jazz
electronic music
expanded tonality
free atonality
Gebrauchsmusik
Gemeinschaftsmusik
happening
Hausmusik
hemitonic music
heteronomous music
honky-tonk
hyperchromaticism
impressionism
inaudible music

internationalism
jazz
Kansas City style
machine music
microtonalism
modality
modern jazz
monodrama
motown
multimedia art
muzak
musique concrète
neo-classicism
neo-modality
neo-romanticism
New Orleans style
non-triadic tonality
panchromaticism
pandiatonicism
pantonality
polytonality
prepared piano
progressive jazz
psychedelic rock
ragtime
rock and roll
rhythm and blues
soul
Spielmusik
stochastic music
strategic music
tape music
third stream
tone poem
twelve-tone music
wallpaper music
Also see listings under **Compositional Techniques, Art Movements.**

Music Groups
American Music Center
American Society of Composers, Authors and Publishers
American Society of University Composers
Broadcast Music Incorporated
Columbia-Princeton Electronic Music Center
EMAMu
French National Radio
International Composers Guild
International Society for Contemporary Music

Jeune France
League of Composers
Once Group
Radio Cologne
Six, Les

Non-Electronic Musical Instruments
acoustical guitar
adapted viola
aleaphone
bamboo marimba
bass guitar
bass marimba
boobams
bonang panembung
brake drum
bull-roarer
Castor and Pollux
chromelodeon I
cloud-chamber bowls
cluster-rake
cocktail drum
diamond marimba
dulcitone
gamelan orchestra
glasses
harmonic canon I
harmonic canon II
hi-hat
intonarumori
kithara I
kithara II
lujon
marimba eroica
mellophonium
sizzle cymbal
spoils of war
surrogate kithara
thunderstick
typophone
vibraphone
whang gun
wind machine
xylomarimba
xylorimba

Performance Practices
bend
blue note
doink
falsetto break
finger drumming
flutter tongue

ghost note
growl
half-valve
multiphonic
nail pizzicato
oboic flux
off note
overblowing
plunger
polinome
riff
rimshot
rip
scordatura
shake
slap pizzicato
slap tongue
smear
snap pizzicato
spill
switch
tonlos
wah-wah
white tone
xyloflux

Rhythm and Meter
added value
additive meter
ametrical rhythm
bimeter
chronometric density
combined meters
cross meter
deci-talas
divisive meter
duration scale
duration series
fractional meter
Hauptrhythmus
heterometric
imbroglio
isorhythm
metrical chord
metrical modulation
multimeter
non-retrogradable rhythm
panrhythm
polymeter
polyrhythm
rhythmic displacement
tempo modulation

time field
time-point set
unequal rhythmic groups
unmeasured meter
variable meter

Scale Resources
Algerian scale
blues scale
comatic scale
dodecuple scale
double harmonic scale
enigmatic scale
gapped scale
heptatonic scale
hexatonic scale
hirajoshi scale
Hungarian scale
infra-diatonic scale
kumoi scale
Lydian minor scale
macrotonal scale
major Locrian scale
modality
multi-octave scale
neapolitan major scale
neapolitan minor scale
octatonic scale
oriental scale
original primitive
overtone scale
pelog scale
pentatonic scale
Prometheus neapolitan scale
Prometheus scale
raga
six-tone scale
stylized primitive scale
sub-infra atonal scale
sub-infra diatonic scale
super Locrian scale
supra-diatonic scale
symmetrical scale
synthetic scale
two-octave scale
whole-tone scale

Twelve-tone Music and Set Theory
aggregate
all-combinatorial set
all-interval set
array
automatism

axis tone
basic cell
bucket notes
combinatoriality
combinatorial set
corresponding segments
cyclic permutation
cyclic transposition
degenerate set
deranged set
derivation technique
duration series
first order set
fourth order set
Grundreihe
hexachord
interchangeability
interval class
invariant
inversion
invertibility
mapping
melodic prototype
multidimensional musical space
nesting
non-combinatorial
numerical notation
octave equivalence
one interval set
operation
ordered pitch classes
ordered set
order number
order-number pitch-number couple
original
partition
permutation
pitch class
pitch number
point of inversion

precompositional aspect
prime
quarternion
retrograde
retrograde-inversion
rotation
secondary set
segmentation
semi-combinatorial set
serialized harmony
serialized melody
serial music
series
set
set-complex
set number
set theory
simultaneity
source set
subset
symmetrical series
telescoping
tetrachord
third order set
time-point set
tone row
total control
total serialization
transformation
transposition
transpositional number
trope
twelve-tone music
twelve-tone row
twelve-tone technique
unordered pitch classes
unordered set
verticalization
vertical melody
vertical permutation

Bibliography

ART MOVEMENTS

Contemporary American Painting and Sculpture. Urbana: University of Illinois Press, 1965.

Fantastic Art, Dada and Surrealism. New York: The Museum of Modern Art, 1936.

Arnason, H. H. *History of Modern Art*. New York: Abrams, 1968.

Baur, John (ed.). *New Art in America*. New York: Graphic Society, 1957.

Brown, Milton W. *American Painting: From the Armory Show to the Depression*. Princeton, N.J.: Princeton University Press, 1955.

Bulliet, C. J. *The Significant Moderns*. New York: Covici Friede, 1936.

Cheney, Sheldon. *Expressionism in Art*. New York: Tudor, 1948.

Fleming, William. *Art, Music and Ideas*. New York: Holt, 1970.

Jean, Marcel. *The History of Surrealist Painting*. New York: Grove, 1960.

Melot, Michel (cataloguer). *The Graphic Works of the Impressionists*. New York: Abrams, 1971.

Newmeyer, Sarah. *Enjoying Modern Art*. New York: Mentor, 1955.

Ponente, Nello. *Modern Painting: Contemporary Trends*. Cleveland: World, 1960.

Richter, Hans. *Dada: Art and Anti-Art*. New York: Abrams, 1970.

Woody, Russell O. *Painting with Synthetic Media*. New York: Reinhold, 1965.

CHANCE MUSIC

Boretz, Benjamin, and Edward Cone (eds.). *Perspectives on Contemporary Music Theory.* New York: Norton, 1972.

Cage, John. *Silence.* Cambridge, Mass.: M.I.T. Press, 1970.

I Ching. Translated by James Legge. New York: Dover, 1963.

Kirby, Michael. *Happenings.* New York: Dutton, 1965.

Xenakis, Iannis. *Formalized Music: Thought and Mathematics in Composition.* Bloomington: Indiana University Press, 1971.

COMPUTER MUSIC

Beauchamp, J. W., and H. Von Foerster (eds.). *Music by Computers.* New York: Wiley, 1969.

Computer Music Newsletter. West Lafayette, Ind.: Music Division of the Creative Arts Department, Purdue University.

Hiller, Lejaren A., Jr., and Leonard M. Isaacson. *Experimental Music: Composition with an Electronic Computer.* New York: McGraw-Hill, 1959.

Hiller, L. J., and A. Leal. *Revised Musicomp Manual.* Urbana: University of Illinois Press, 1966.

Lefkoff, Gerald (ed.). *Computer Applications in Music.* Morgantown: West Virginia University Library, 1967.

Lincoln, Harry B. (ed.). *The Computer and Music.* Ithaca, N.Y.: Cornell University Press, 1970.

Mathews, Max V. *Technology of Computer Music.* Cambridge, Mass.: M.I.T. Press, 1969.

Reichardt, Jasia. *Cybernetic Serendipity: The Computer and the Arts.* New York: Praeger, 1969.

Rodgers, Harold A. *Dictionary of Data Processing Terms.* New York: Funk & Wagnalls, 1970.

irmer—A Lexicon   AA's   8on8 cal x 21X   ro-mark 40373-G   DickH-4

ELECTRONIC MUSIC

Cross, Lowell. *A Bibliography of Electronic Music.* Toronto: University of Toronto Press, 1966.

Crowhurst, Norman H. *Electronic Musical Instruments.* Blue Ridge Summit, Pa.: Tab Books, 1971.

Douglas, Alan. *Electronic Music Production.* London: Pitman, 1973.

Douglas, Alan. *The Electronic Musical Instrument Manual.* London: Pitman, 1968.

Judd, F. C. *Electronics in Music.* London: Spearman, 1972.

Music Educators Journal. Washington, D.C.: Music Educators National Conference, November, 1968.

Music Educators Journal. Washington, D.C.: Music Educators Conference, January, 1971.

Numus-West. Mercer Island, Wash.: 1972– .

Schwartz, Elliott S. *Electronic Music: A Listener's Guide.* New York: Praeger, 1973.

Strange, Allen. *Electronic Music.* Dubuque, Iowa: William C. Brown, 1972.

Tremaine, Howard M. *The Audio Cyclopedia.* Indianapolis, Ind.: Howard W. Sams, 1959.

Trythall, Gilbert. *Principles and Practice of Electronic Music.* New York: Grosset & Dunlap, 1974.

FILM MUSIC

Dolan, Robert Emmett. *Music in Modern Media.* New York: G. Schirmer, 1967.

Hagen, Earle. *Scoring for Films.* New York: E. D. J. Music, 1971.

London, Kurt. *Film Music.* London: Faber & Faber, 1970.

JAZZ, ROCK, AND POPULAR MUSIC

Baker, David. *Jazz Improvisation.* Chicago: Maher, 1969.

Coker, Jerry. *Improvising Jazz.* Englewood Cliffs, N.J.: Prentice-Hall, 1964.

Dankworth, Avril. *Jazz: An Introduction to Its Musical Basis.* London: Oxford University Press, 1968.

Gold, Robert. *A Jazz Lexicon.* New York: Knopf, 1964.

Martin, John, and William Fritz. *Listening to Jazz.* Fresno, Calif.: Fresno University Press, 1970.

Ricigliano, Daniel. *Popular and Jazz Harmony.* New York: Donato, 1967.

Robinson, Richard. *Electric Rock.* New York: Pyramid, 1971.

Roxon, Lillian. *Rock Encyclopedia.* New York: Grosset & Dunlap, 1969.

Russo, William. *Composing for the Jazz Orchestra.* Chicago: University of Chicago Press, 1961.

Schiffman, Jack. *Uptown: The Story of Harlem's Apollo Theatre.* New York: Cowles, 1971.

Schuller, Gunther. *Early Jazz.* New York: Oxford University Press, 1968.

Stambler, Irving. *Encyclopedia of Popular Music.* New York: St. Martin's Press, 1965.

Stambler, Irving, and Grelun Landon. *Encyclopedia of Folk, Country and Western Music.* New York: St. Martin's Press, 1969.

Stearns, Marshall. *The Story of Jazz.* New York: New American Library, 1956.

Tanner, Paul, and Maurice Gerow. *A Study of Jazz.* Dubuque, Iowa: William C. Brown, 1964.

MUSIC NOTATION

Donato, Anthony. *Preparing Music Manuscript*. Englewood Cliffs, N.J.: Prentice-Hall, 1963.

Karkoschka, Erhard. *Notation in New Music*. New York: Praeger, 1972.

Read, Gardner. *Music Notation: A Manual of Modern Practice*. Boston: Allyn & Bacon, 1969.

THEORY AND ANALYSIS

Cooper, Paul. *Perspectives in Music Theory*. New York: Dodd-Mead, 1973.

Cooper, Grosvenor, and Leonard Meyer. *The Rhythmic Structure of Music*. Chicago: University of Chicago Press, 1960.

Cowell, Henry. *New Musical Resources*. New York: Something Else Press, 1969.

Dallin, Leon. *Techniques of Twentieth Century Composition*. 2nd ed. Dubuque, Iowa: William C. Brown, 1971.

Forte, Allen. *Contemporary Tone-Structures*. New York: Columbia University Press, 1955.

Hanson, Howard. *Harmonic Materials of Modern Music*. New York: Appleton-Century-Crofts, 1960.

Hindemith, Paul. *The Craft of Musical Composition*. New York: Associated Music, 1945.

Jones, Robert C. *A Glossary of Theoretical Terms Used in Selected Writings in English about Twentieth-Century Music*. Ann Arbor, Mich.: University Microfilms, 1966.

Journal of Music Theory. Vol. 1, March 1957. New Haven, Conn.: Yale School of Music.

Lang, Paul H. (ed.). *Problems of Modern Music.* New York: Norton, 1962.

LaRue, Jan. *Guidelines for Style Analysis.* New York: Norton, 1970.

Marquis, G. Welton. *Twentieth-Century Music Idioms.* Englewood Cliffs, N.J.: Prentice-Hall, 1964.

Persichetti, Vincent. *Twentieth-Century Harmony.* New York: Norton, 1961.

Perspectives of New Music. Vol. 1, Fall 1962. Princeton, N.J.: Princeton University Press.

Reihe, Die. Volumes 1–8. (English Translation). Bryn Mawr, Pa.: T. Presser, 1955– .

Reti, Rudolf. *Tonality–Atonality–Pantonality.* New York: Macmillan, 1958.

Salzer, Felix. *Structural Hearing.* New York: Boni, 1952.

Schenker, Heinrich. *Five Graphic Music Analyses.* New York: Dover, 1967.

Schillinger, Joseph. *The Schillinger System of Musical Composition.* New York: C. Fischer, 1946.

Searle, Humphrey. *Twentieth Century Counterpoint.* New York: DeGraff, 1954.

Slonimsky, Nicolas. *Thesaurus of Scales and Melodic Patterns.* New York: Coleman-Ross, 1947.

Source; Music of the Avant-Garde. Vol. 1, Jan. 1967. Davis, California.

Ulehla, Ludmila. *Contemporary Harmony: Romanticism Through the Twelve-Tone Row.* New York: Free Press, 1966.

Vincent, John N. *The Diatonic Modes in Modern Music.* New York: Mills, 1951.

Yassar, Joseph. *A Theory of Evolving Tonality.* New York: American Library of Musicology, 1932.

NON-ELECTRONIC MUSICAL INSTRUMENTS

Partch, Harry. *Genesis of a Music*. Madison: University of Wisconsin Press, 1949.

Reed, Owen, and Joel Leach. *Scoring for Percussion*. Englewood Cliffs, N.J.: Prentice-Hall, 1969.

Sachs, Curt. *The History of Musical Instruments*. New York: Norton, 1940.

TWELVE-TONE MUSIC

Basart, Ann. *Serial Music: A Classified Bibliography of Writings on Twelve-Tone and Electronic Music*. Berkeley: University of California Press, 1961.

Brindle, Reginald Smith. *Serial Composition*. London: Oxford University Press, 1972.

Perle, George. *Serial Composition and Atonality*. Berkeley: University of California Press, 1968.

Rochberg, George. *The Hexachord and Its Relation to the Twelve-Tone Row*. Bryn Mawr, Pa.: Presser, 1955.

Rufer, Josef. *Composition with Twelve Notes Related Only to One Another*. New York: Macmillan, 1954.

Webern, Anton. *The Path to the New Music*. Bryn Mawr, Pa.: Presser, 1963.

Wellesz, Egon. *Arnold Schoenberg*. New York: Dutton, 1925.

Wellesz, Egon. *The Origins of Schoenberg's Twelve-Tone System*. Washington, D.C.: U.S. Government Printing Office, 1958.

GENERAL REFERENCE

Apel, Willi. *Harvard Dictionary of Music.* Cambridge: The Belknap Press of Harvard University Press, 1969.

Austin, William W. *Music in the 20th Century.* New York: Norton, 1966.

Collaer, Paul. *A History of Modern Music.* New York: Grosset & Dunlap, 1961.

Cope, David. *New Directions in Music.* Dubuque, Iowa: William C. Brown, 1971.

Copland, Aaron. *The New Music 1900–1960.* New York: Norton, 1968.

Demuth, Norman. *Musical Trends in the 20th Century.* London: Rockliff, 1952.

Deri, Otto. *Exploring Twentieth-Century Music.* New York: Holt, 1968.

Ewen, David. *Modern Music.* New York: Chilton, 1969.

Hansen, Peter S. *Twentieth Century Music.* Boston: Allyn & Bacon, 1967.

Hartog, Howard (ed.). *European Music in the Twentieth Century.* New York: Praeger, 1957.

Hines, Robert Stephan (ed.). *The Orchestral Composer's Point of View: Essays on Twentieth-Century Music by Those Who Wrote It.* Norman: University of Oklahoma Press, 1970.

Laing, David. *The Sound of Our Time.* Chicago: Quadrangle Books, 1969.

Machlis, Joseph. *Introduction to Contemporary Music.* New York: Norton, 1961.

Meyers, Rollo H. *Twentieth Century Music.* London: Calder & Boyars, 1968.

Mitchell, Donald. *The Language of Modern Music.* London: Faber & Faber, 1966.

Peyser, Joan. *The New Music.* New York: Dell, 1971.

Rossi, Nick, and Robert A. Choate. *Music of Our Time.* Boston: Crescendo, 1969.

Russolo, Luigi. *The Art of Noise.* Trans. Robert Fillion. New York: Something Else Press, 1967.

Salazar, Adolfo. *Music in Our Time.* New York: Norton, 1946.

Salzman, Eric. *Twentieth-Century Music: An Introduction.* Englewood Cliffs, N.J.: Prentice-Hall, 1967.

Schwartz, Elliott, and Barney Childs (eds.). *Contemporary Composers on Contemporary Music.* New York: Holt, 1967.

Slonimsky, Nicolas. *Music Since 1900.* New York: Scribner, 1971.

Stuckenschmidt, H. H. *Twentieth Century Music.* New York: McGraw-Hill, 1969.

Vinton, John (ed.). *Dictionary of Contemporary Music.* New York: Dutton, 1974.

Wennerstrom, Mary H. *Anthology of Twentieth-Century Music.* New York: Appleton-Century-Crofts, 1969.

Yates, Peter. *Twentieth Century Music.* New York: Pantheon, 1967.